NELSON GRAPHY

Interactions

Teacher's Handbook

5th Edition

CATHERINE HURST AND NICHOLAS ROWLES

DAVID WAUGH AND TONY BUSHELL

OXFORD UNIVERSITY PRESS

OXFORD
UNIVERSITY PRESS

Great Clarendon Street, Oxford, OX2 6DP, United Kingdom

Oxford University Press is a department of the University of Oxford. It furthers the University's objective of excellence in research, scholarship, and education by publishing worldwide. Oxford is a registered trade mark of Oxford University Press in the UK and in certain other countries

© Oxford University Press 2014

Authors: Catherine Hurst and Nicholas Rowles

The moral rights of the authors have been asserted

First published in 2012

This edition 2014

All rights reserved. No part of this publication may be reproduced, stored in a retrieval system, or transmitted, in any form or by any means, without the prior permission in writing of Oxford University Press, or as expressly permitted by law, by licence or under terms agreed with the appropriate reprographics rights organization. Enquiries concerning reproduction outside the scope of the above should be sent to the Rights Department, Oxford University Press, at the address above.

You must not circulate this work in any other form and you must impose this same condition on any acquirer

British Library Cataloguing in Publication Data
Data available

978-1-40 852732-0

10 9 8 7 6 5 4 3 2 1

Paper used in the production of this book is a natural, recyclable product made from wood grown in sustainable forests.
The manufacturing process conforms to the environmental regulations of the country of origin.

Printed in Spain by Graphycems

Acknowledgements

The publishers would like to thank the following for permission to use photographs and other copyright material:

Illustrations by Kathy Baxendale, Nick Hawken, Angela Knowles, Gordon Lawson, GreenGate Publishing Services, Richard Morris, David Russell, Tim Smith, John Yorke

Cover photographs: FTFoxfoto/Fotalia; Vision/Fotalia; Rainer Albeiz//Shutterstock; TA Crafts/iStockphoto

Every effort has been made to contact copyright holders of material reproduced in this book. Any omissions will be rectified in subsequent printings if notice is given to the publisher.

Links to third party websites are provided by Oxford in good faith and for information only. Oxford disclaims any responsibility for the materials contained in any third party website referenced in this work.

Contents

4 China – the emerging nation

5 International development

6 Key skills: enquiries

Appendices

How to use this book

This Teacher's Handbook has been written to accompany the *Nelson Key Geography Interactions* pupil book. It is intended to provide:

- full support for newly qualified teachers
- ideas for experienced, but busy, geography teachers
- ideas for experienced teachers who are not geographers.

Its aim is to provide succinct, at-a-glance information specifically to:

- help provide teachers plan and deliver high-quality geography lessons
- provide support, ideas, and suggestions for the use of additional resources
- explain the geographical content of each unit
- provide answers to the activities in the pupil book.

Where items are included here as suggestions, i.e. the Skills builders and Differentiation suggestions, they are intended to be just that. They are not meant to be prescriptive. You may want to use them as they stand, or they may spark off other, better, ideas that you can use.

Pupil Book pages 6–7

What factors affect climate?

About this spread

This spread begins by revising the difference between weather and climate. Pupils then need to understand how latitude, distance from the sea, prevailing winds and relief (altitude) affect climate. This first spread of the unit is all theory, which is dealt with through the use of simplified, annotated diagrams. Pupils should then be able to understand what follows in the rest of the unit.

Learning outcomes

By the end of this spread pupils should be able to:

- explain the difference between weather and climate
- name four factors that affect climate
- draw diagrams to show how different factors affect climate.

Key vocabulary

- **weather**
- **climate**
- **latitude**
- **prevailing wind**
- **relief (altitude)**

Learning objectives

On this spread pupils should learn:

- that climate is influenced by latitude, distance from the sea, prevailing winds and relief (altitude)
- about how the different factors affect climate.

Skills builder

Pupils need to be able to use and understand the correct geographical terminology, for the topic they are studying, which some pupils may find difficult to grasp or remember. They can look up technical terms in the glossary in the pupil book, or they can produce their own dictionary of key vocabulary. You could also help pupils by displaying the terms around the classroom, along with their definitions. At GCSE level, pupils will achieve higher grades if they are able to use the correct, appropriate terminology.

Further discussion suggestions

- Is the climate of a place its average weather over: **a** 15 years, **b** 30 years, **c** 35 years, **d** 40 years, **e** 50 years?
- How does the sea moderate Britain's climate?
- Why is the south-east of Britain warmer and drier than the north-west of Britain?

Answers to activities

1 Weather is the day-to-day condition of the atmosphere. It includes things like temperature, precipitation and wind. Climate is the average of the weather for a given place taken over many years (for example, 30 years).

2 a, b and **c**

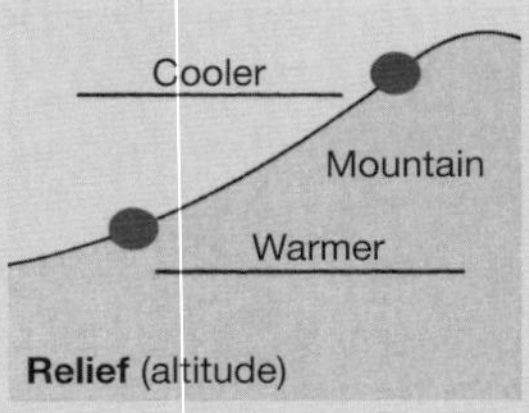

Temperature decreases with height.

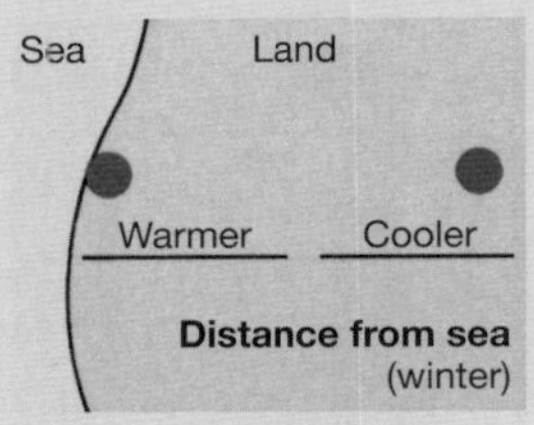

The sea keeps coastal places warm.

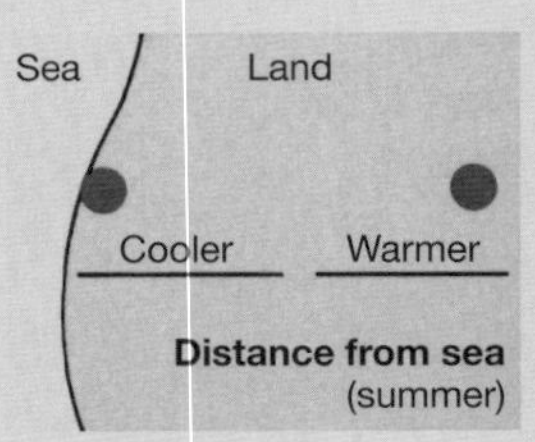

The sea keeps coastal places cool.

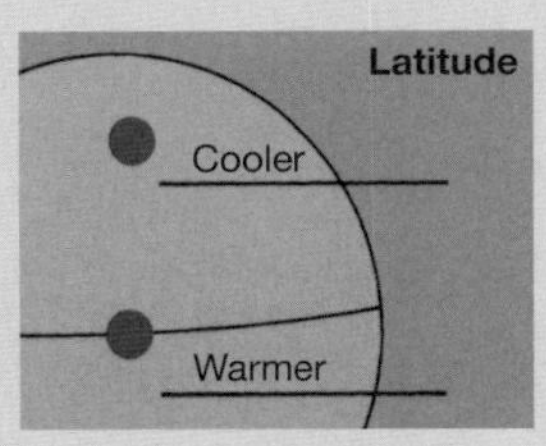

Places near the Equator are warmer because of the overhead sun.

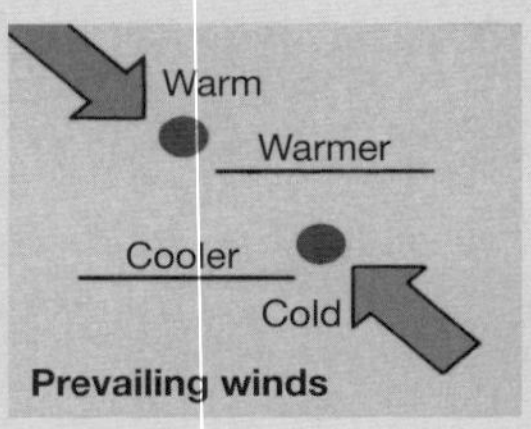

Temperature is affected by the direction from which the wind comes.

3

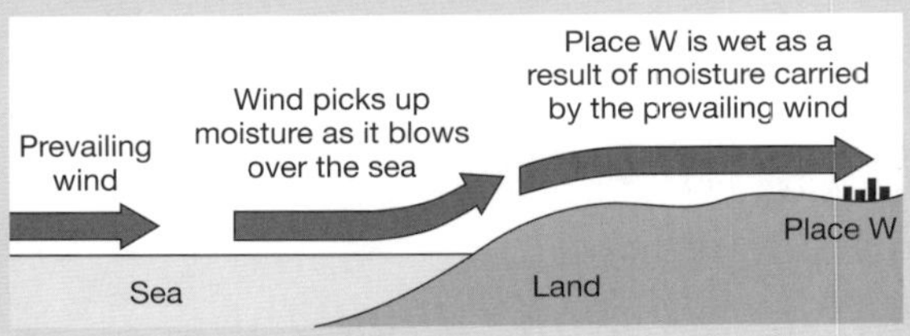

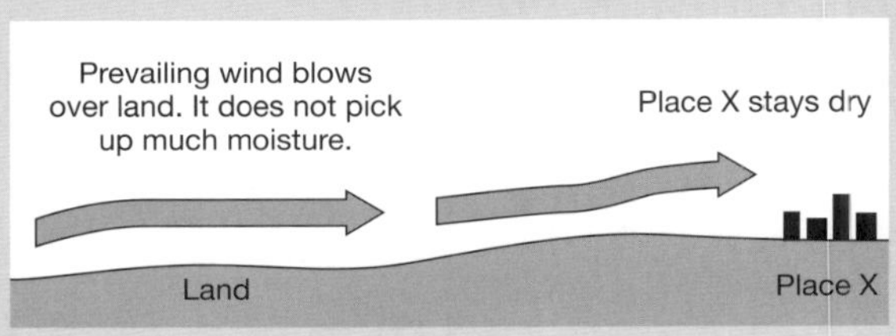

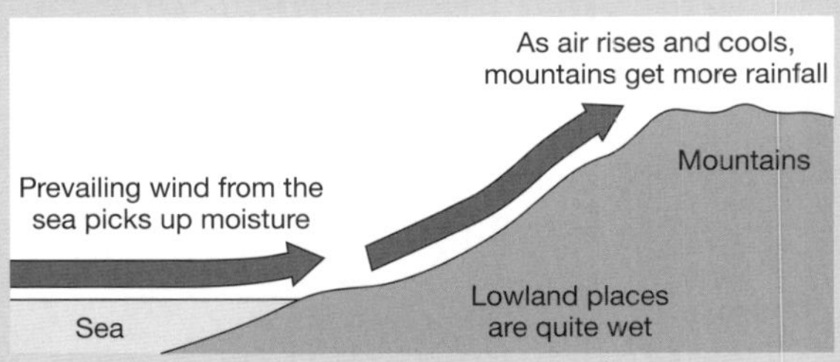

a Prevailing winds can bring wet weather to places if they blow over the sea and pick up moisture – as the diagram shows.

b Prevailing winds can bring dry weather to places if they blow over the land – as the diagram shows.

c Mountains usually get more rain than lowland areas for the reason shown in the diagram.

Pupil Book pages 8–9

What is Britain's climate?

About this spread

This spread applies the theory from the previous spread to Britain's climate. It is important that pupils can understand why Britain has cool summers, mild winters and rainfall throughout the year. They should also try to appreciate what we mean when we talk about 'a warm summer day', a 'mild winter', 'today's temperature of 10 °C is average for the time of year'. Pupils need to have this feel for their own climate if they are going to make meaningful comparisons with other types of climate. This spread provides an opportunity to revisit the use and understanding of climate graphs introduced in *Nelson Key Geography Foundations*, and to ensure that pupils are aware of contrasting climates in other parts of the world.

Learning outcomes

By the end of this spread pupils should be able to:

- interpret a climate graph showing Britain's climate
- describe Britain's climate
- name other places in the world that have a British-type climate
- understand that other parts of the world have very different climates.

Key vocabulary

- **frontal rainfall**
- **convectional rainfall**
- **relief rainfall**

Learning objectives

On this spread pupils should learn:

- that Britain has cool summers, mild winters and rainfall throughout the year
- that some other parts of the world have a climate similar to Britain
- that other parts of the world have very different climates.

Skills builder

One of the skills that pupils need to develop in geography is the ability to use and interpret a wide range of graphs and diagrams. They need to be able to draw them and interpret what they show. On this spread, pupils use an annotated graph to learn about Britain's climate and the reasons for it. Pupils meet climate graphs again on page 12 (equatorial climate) and page 16 (Mediterranean climate). If pupils continue to study geography at GCSE, they are likely to come across climate graphs again, when studying, for example, the climate of the UK, extreme climates in different parts of the world, or climates of different places when studying tourism.

Further discussion suggestions

- Why is Britain's climate type called 'maritime'?
- Where would you find a continental-type climate and what would it be like?
- Why is much of Kenya sunny, dry and not too hot for most of the year, despite being situated on the Equator?

Answers to activities

1 The British Isles have **cool** summers, **mild** winters and **rainfall** throughout the year.

2 Pupils are asked to name four places in the world that have the same type of climate as Britain. They should choose from map C on page 8 of the pupil book, which includes:

- North-west USA and west Canada
- Southern Chile
- North-west Europe
- Tasmania
- South Island of New Zealand.

3 The correct statements are as follows.

- Summers are cool because Britain is a long way from the Equator.
- Winters are mild due to warm winds blowing from the sea.
- Rain falls all year because winds blow from the sea.
- Britain gets frontal and relief rainfall all year, and convectional rainfall in summer.

Pupil Book pages 10–11

What are ecosystems?

About this spread

This spread introduces pupils to ecosystems. It explains what they are and the links between the different elements in an ecosystem. Pupils should be aware that if one element of an ecosystem changes, it can have a major impact on the other parts of the ecosystem. This spread uses a map of the world to show the global distribution of the world's main ecosystems, or biomes. This page looks at two of these in more detail – tropical rainforest (and equatorial climate) and Mediterranean climate and vegetation.

Learning outcomes

By the end of this spread pupils should be able to:

- explain what an ecosystem is and how the elements of an ecosystem are linked
- describe the global distribution of tropical rainforests and Mediterranean ecosystems
- give examples of how ecosystems can be damaged by human activities.

Key vocabulary

- **ecosystem**
- **rainforest**
- **biome**
- **vegetation**
- **acid rain**

Learning objectives

On this spread pupils should learn:

- about the elements that make up an ecosystem and the way they are linked
- that ecosystems can vary in scale and from place to place
- that human activities can change and destroy ecosystems.

Skills builder

In geography, pupils need to be able to identify patterns on maps and describe distributions – it is a key skill. Map B on page 11 shows the global distribution of the world's major ecosystems. Pupils need to be aware that this distribution has not happened by accident. As the text mentions, the vegetation found in different ecosystems or biomes is largely determined by climatic factors such as temperature, rainfall, sunshine and wind. Understanding this will allow pupils to explain the distribution of different ecosystems, as well as to describe the distribution.

Further discussion suggestions

- Which of the following is not a biome: **a** tundra, **b** a pond, **c** desert, **d** grassland?
- What problems does acid rain cause in Scandinavia?
- What effect does extensive logging have on Canada's coniferous forest?

Answers to activities

1 a The environment is the natural or physical surroundings where plants and animals live.

b The non-living environment includes rocks, soil, the air and climate.

c The living environment includes animals, birds, fish, insects and people.

d An ecosystem is the interaction of plants and animals with their non-living surroundings.

e A natural ecosystem is a community of plants and animals unaffected by human activity.

f A biome is a large ecosystem such as a desert or tropical rainforest.

2 a Pupils' answers will vary but the following may be among their answers: pond, hedgerow, woodland, meadow.

b The links in a meadow ecosystem would be:

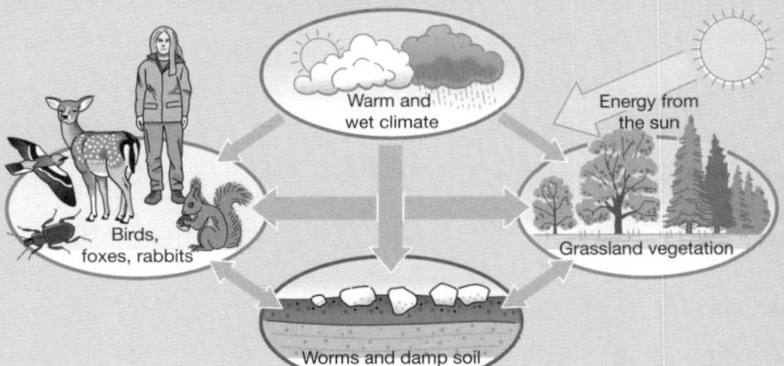

3 a and **b**

Headline	Acid rain damage hits Scandinavian forests	Arctic oil spill threatens caribou grazing land	Woodland cleared for Lake District leisure complex	Kenyan wildlife threatened by farmers ploughing and overgrazing the land	Problems for Brazil as miners and loggers clear more forest	Global warming blamed for spread of desert
Biome	Coniferous forest	Tundra	Deciduous woodland	Grassland	Tropical rainforest	Desert
How plants, animals or people might benefit or suffer from the changes, with reasons	Trees will die because acid rain is a form of air pollution.	Caribou might be unable to feed as oil will pollute their grazing land.	The woodland ecosystem of plants and animals will be destroyed. People might benefit from the development of a leisure complex, but will lose the natural environment.	Wildlife will lose their habitat as farmers plough land for farming. Overgrazing will destroy natural vegetation and mean there is less food available for wildlife.	Rainforest will be destroyed, animals will lose their habitats, indigenous people will lose farming and hunting land.	As deserts spread, plants, animals and people will lose out if they cannot adapt to the changing environment.

Pupil Book pages 12–13

What is the equatorial climate?

About this spread

This spread begins by summarising the equatorial climate by means of a graph. The graph allows pupils to make a straightforward comparison with Britain's climate on page 8 of the pupil book. This is followed by a description of a typical day's weather for a place on the Equator. There are no seasons in this part of the world and the weather for one day is very similar to that of the next. Map D on page 13 locates those places with an equatorial climate. Finally, a photo of the snow-covered landscape of Mount Kenya on the Equator illustrates the effect of altitude on the climate of places that have the same latitude.

Learning outcomes

By the end of this spread pupils should be able to:

- describe the equatorial climate and pattern of weather
- describe the location of places with an equatorial climate
- describe the differences between an equatorial climate and Britain's climate.

Key vocabulary

- **equatorial climate**
- **altitude**

Learning objectives

On this spread pupils should learn:

- about the main features of a typical equatorial climate
- about the global distribution of places with an equatorial climate
- about the effect that altitude has on climate.

Skills builder

Activity 5 on page 13 of the pupil book asks pupils to describe the differences between two types of climate – an equatorial climate (which they have studied on this spread) and Britain's climate (which they studied on pages 8–9). This may sound quite simple but, in order to answer this question, pupils need to be able to interpret the climate graphs for both climates and understand the associated text. In order to describe the differences, pupils have to compare the climates and look for similarities and differences. If pupils continue to study geography at GCSE level, they will come across many instances where they are asked to compare different things: climates, responses to natural disasters in different countries, levels of development in different countries, and so on. Therefore, they need to understand what the term 'compare' means.

Further discussion suggestions

- How does daily torrential rain affect the nutrients in tropical rainforest soil?
- Why is the daily temperature range of an equatorial climate greater than the annual temperature range?
- What are the 'doldrums'?

Answers to activities

1 The equatorial climate is hot and wet all year. Rainfall is heavy and falls during most afternoons. The weather for each day of the year is very similar.

2 It is mainly found between latitudes 5 °N and 5 °S of the Equator.

It is found in the Amazon Basin in South America and in the Congo Basin in Africa.

3 **a** January temperature is 27 °C.

July temperature is 28 °C.

b It is hot throughout the year as this type of climate is found in equatorial regions where the sun is overhead all year.

4 **a** The total annual rainfall is 1,800 mm.

b Some places near the Equator have snow lying all the year because they are at a high altitude. The higher the altitude means the lower the temperature. Temperature decreases by 1 °C for every 100 metres in height (above sea level).

5 Pupils are asked to describe three differences between an equatorial climate and Britain's climate. Differences include the following.

- The equatorial climate is hot all year, with no seasons. Britain's climate varies in temperature, with cool summers and mild winters – Britain has distinct seasons.
- Both climates have rain all year round, but the equatorial climate has about twice the amount of rain than Britain. It has significantly less rain in the months between June and September.
- In areas with an equatorial climate the weather pattern tends to be the same every day. The weather associated with Britain's climate is far more variable.
- The equatorial climate has convectional rainfall; Britain's climate has frontal, relief and convectional rainfall.

Pupil Book pages 14–15

What are tropical rainforests?

About this spread

This spread describes the tropical rainforest and uses a large drawing to show how the vegetation in the rainforest has adapted to the equatorial climate. It also looks at the vast range of wildlife that is found in the rainforest. Activity 2 asks pupils to describe how the wildlife has adapted to living in the hot, wet forest environment. It might be worth spending some time making sure that pupils understand the term 'adapted', as they will come across it again when looking at Mediterranean vegetation on pages 18 and 19.

Learning outcomes

By the end of this spread pupils should be able to:

- describe the main features of a tropical rainforest
- understand that the tropical rainforest is an important resource that has more trees and wildlife than anywhere else on earth
- describe how plants have adapted to the equatorial climate.

Key vocabulary

- **tropical rainforest**
- **hardwood**
- **adapt**
- **emergents**
- **lianas**
- **buttress roots**
- **canopy**
- **deforestation**

Learning objectives

On this spread pupils should learn:

- that tropical rainforests grow in areas with an equatorial climate
- how vegetation in a tropical rainforest has adapted to the equatorial climate
- that rainforests are an important resource.

Skills builder

The material on this spread not only tells pupils what tropical rainforests are and what they are like, but also provides an opportunity for pupils to develop their thinking skills. Page 15 of the pupil book tells pupils that over half of our known medicines have come from tropical rainforests, and also that tropical rainforests are under threat from deforestation and other human activities.

Rainforests have a value both as a resource that can be exploited and used up, e.g. as in logging, or as a resource that can be used in its natural state to provide medicines, an environment for ecotourism, and so on. This material allows pupils to see the link between human action and the environment. At GCSE level, pupils will achieve more highly if they are able to recognise and understand complex relationships between people and the environment.

Further discussion suggestions

- Why does the destruction of rainforests have a global effect?
- Why may tropical countries where rainforests are found want to continue to cut them down?
- How can the destruction of the rainforests be publicised?

Answers to activities

1 1 = under-canopy
2 = shrub layer
3 = buttress roots
4 = little undergrowth
5 = lianas
6 = main canopy
7 = branchless trunks

2 Pupils' answers will vary but should be along the following lines:

As the trees are so tall the monkeys have developed the use of their tails to help them climb up to get the fruit from the high branches. The jaguar's coat forms a camouflage so they are difficult to see in the dense forest. The orchids, because they do not grow on the ground, are able to get moisture from the trees that they are growing from.

3 **a** The trees need to grow tall so that they can get sunlight.

b Buttress roots are needed to support the trees.

c There is little undergrowth as sunlight cannot penetrate down to ground level.

d Plants grow quickly because the growing season is continuous – it is always hot and wet, with high temperatures and heavy rainfall.

Pupil Book pages 16–17

What is a Mediterranean climate?

About this spread

This spread looks at the Mediterranean climate. It begins with a climate graph of the Mediterranean climate, which allows pupils to compare it with the equatorial climate on pages 12–13 of the pupil book and Britain's climate on page 8. It explains that the Mediterranean has two very different seasons – hot, dry summers and warm, wet winters – and explains why this is. A world map shows those parts of the world that have a Mediterranean climate.

Learning outcomes

By the end of this spread pupils should be able to:

- interpret a climate graph for the Mediterranean climate
- explain why Mediterranean summers are hot and dry, and winters are warm and wet
- name different parts of the world that have a Mediterranean climate.

Key vocabulary

- **Mediterranean climate**

Learning objectives

On this spread pupils should learn:

- about the main features of a Mediterranean climate
- the causes of the seasonal variations in the climate in Mediterranean regions
- the location of places with a Mediterranean climate.

Skills builder

This spread will give further opportunities for pupils to construct and interpret climate graphs. The interpretation of the graph can be helped by the construction of a living graph where the different human activities such as farming and tourism can be linked to the different months/seasons of the year.

Further discussion suggestions

- Why does the prevailing wind in areas with a Mediterranean climate reverse direction when summer turns to winter?
- What effect does the Mistral have on the Mediterranean climate in the south of France?
- How many hours of sunshine do Los Angeles (USA), Santiago (Chile), Rome (Italy) and Cape Town (South Africa) receive on average each year?

Answers to activities

1 California, Central Chile, around the Mediterranean Sea, South Africa, south-west Australia, south-east Australia.

2 **a** and **b**

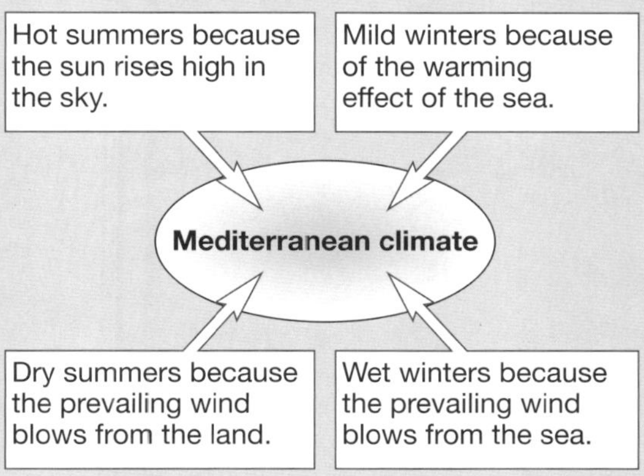

3 **a** The temperature in January is 9 °C. The temperature in July is 28 °C.

b 400 mm rain falls in an average year.

4 **a** Many British people go on holiday to a place with a Mediterranean climate in the summer because the weather should be warm and dry.

b Some elderly British people go to a place with a Mediterranean climate in winter because the temperatures are higher than they would be back in the UK. This means that they do not have to spend a lot of their pensions on central heating and other ways of keeping warm.

Pupil Book pages 18–19

What is Mediterranean vegetation like?

About this spread

This spread looks at what Mediterranean vegetation is like and how it has adapted to the seasonal climate pattern of hot, dry summers and warm, wet winters. A large drawing on page 18 of the pupil book shows some of these adaptations. The spread then looks at how the vegetation has been changed by people. Originally, land around the Mediterranean Sea would have been covered in forest, but now the main form of vegetation is scrub. This change in vegetation has been mainly caused by the activity of people who settled in the region and their grazing animals.

Learning outcomes

By the end of this spread pupils should be able to:

- name different plants found in the Mediterranean
- describe how Mediterranean vegetation has had to adapt to the hot, dry summers and warm, wet winters
- list ways in which the vegetation in the Mediterranean has been affected by human activities.

Key vocabulary

- **scrub**
- **dormant**

Learning objectives

On this spread pupils should learn:

- about the main types of vegetation found in the Mediterranean region
- how the vegetation has adapted to the Mediterranean climate
- how vegetation in the Mediterranean region has been affected by human activity.

Skills builder

The material on this spread allows pupils to see the link between human actions and the impact of those actions on the environment. At GCSE level, pupils will be expected to recognise and understand relationships between people and the environment, identify and evaluate problems and issues, and make geographical decisions about them.

Further discussion suggestions

- Scrub vegetation growing in a Mediterranean climate is known in France as *maquis* or *garrigue*. What is its name in: **a** California, **b** Chile, **c** Italy, **d** South Africa, **e** Australia?
- How can fire benefit some plants that grow in a Mediterranean climate?

Answers to activities

1 Pupils are asked to name six Mediterranean plants. Those mentioned on this spread include: pine trees; cypress trees; cork oak; thorn bush; lavender; thyme; rosemary.

2 **a** Mediterranean plants grow mainly in the winter as this is when water is available and temperatures are warm, rather than too hot.

b They only grow very slowly in the summer as there is little rain, so little water is available, and it is very hot.

3 Pupils are asked for three ways in which Mediterranean vegetation has adapted to survive in the hot, dry summer. These include having:

- small, thin, waxy or leathery leaves to reduce moisture loss
- thick bark as protection against the heat
- a quick life cycle to fit the short growing season
- long roots to reach underground water
- leaves that roll up tightly to reduce moisture loss
- seeds that have thick 'coats' as protection against the heat.

4 Pupils are asked for three ways in which the natural Mediterranean vegetation has been altered by human activity. These include:

- grazing animals – herds of sheep and goats have eaten young trees
- trees have been cut down for building houses and ships
- trees have been used as fuel
- forest fires (some started deliberately).

5

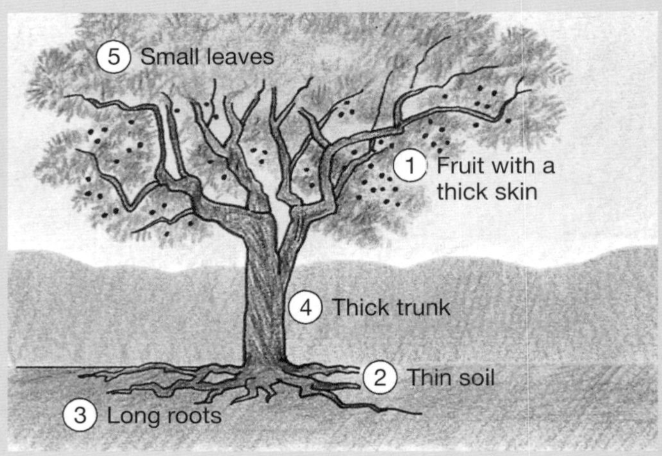

Pupil Book pages 20–21

What is a hot desert climate?

About this spread

In this spread pupils will learn how the factors of latitude, distance from the sea and the prevailing winds explain why hot deserts experience hot dry conditions. It also explains why there is such a large difference between the day and night temperatures. The geographical distribution of this biome is described giving the pupils the opportunity to gain familiarity of the names of the major hot deserts of the world. It builds on the factors influencing climate which reinforces the work already covered on Britain's climate. It gives a simple introduction to the importance of atmospheric circulation and global wind systems.

Learning outcomes

By the end of this spread pupils should be able to:

- describe the main features of the hot desert climate
- describe and name the locations of places with a hot desert climate
- explain the factors responsible for temperature and rainfall pattern experienced in hot deserts.

Key vocabulary

- **hot desert**
- **desert climate**

Learning objectives

On this spread pupils should learn:

- about the main features of a hot desert climate
- about the global distribution of places with a hot desert climate
- about the factors responsible for the temperature and rainfall conditions experienced in hot deserts.

Skills builder

This spread gives the opportunity for pupils to increase their sense of place by an appreciation of the names and locations of the world's hot deserts. It also reinforces the importance of the word 'compare' which, at GCSE level, is largely concerned with similarities, as opposed to 'contrast' where the differences are emphasised more. Pupils could compare a temperate climate with a hot desert climate. The candidates should be taught to recognise patterns or trends by giving a general overall comment about the climate, quoting some representative figures and noting any exceptions to the general pattern.

Further discussion suggestions

- Why is a blanket required if you plan to sleep in a tent in a hot desert?
- Why do people who live in hot deserts wear clothing like that illustrated in photo B on page 20?
- Are all hot deserts covered with sand?

Answers to activities

1 **a** Africa: two from Sahara, Namib and Kalahari.

Americas: two from Sonoran, Chihuahuan, Sechura and Atacama.

b They are mainly on the western sides of the continent where the winds are blowing from land to sea.

c Two from:

They are in the centre or on the western side of continents.

They are usually between latitudes 10° and 30° north or south of the Equator.

They are where the prevailing winds come from dry land.

2 The hot desert is very **hot** in **summer** and during the **day**. It is much colder in **winter** and during the **night**. The amounts of cloud and rainfall are **small**.

3

In hot desserts → air is descending → air gets warmer → evaporates and gives cloudless skies

4 **a** The temperature is 12 °C in January; the temperature is 35 °C in July.

b The sun is high in the sky and there are no clouds to shade the land.

c The total rainfall in a year is 100 mm.

d Winds blow from a dry area. The air is descending and so it gets warmer, causes evaporation and so there is little moisture to fall as rain.

Pupil Book pages 22–23

How do plants and wildlife survive in hot deserts?

About this spread

In this spread pupils learn about the flora and fauna of the hot deserts and how they have adapted in order to survive in such a hostile environment. The pupils are given the opportunity to think how a person in the desert has to be prepared, as hot deserts do not have features which give natural protection from the elements.

Learning objectives

On this spread pupils should learn:

- the ways plants and animals have evolved features that allow them to survive in hot desert conditions
- what a human has to do in order to survive hot desert conditions.

Learning outcomes

By the end of this spread pupils should be able to:

- name the main features of desert vegetation and wildlife
- explain how these features give them protection from desert conditions
- describe the clothing that is necessary to cope with the high sunshine totals and high temperatures of a hot desert.

Key vocabulary

- **adapt**
- **drought**
- **dormant**
- **cactus**

Skills builder

This spread shows pupils that plants and animals can adapt to extreme conditions. It allows them to appreciate that humans are often less adaptable and therefore have to take special measures in order to survive. The pupils are given more practice in annotating photographs. Get pupils to consider what an animal may look like if it had to survive in a climate of extreme temperature and/or rainfall. Higher-ability pupils could be given an extra factor such as relief or altitude to take into consideration.

Further discussion suggestions

- Which desert plants could help a person who is lost in a hot desert and is desperate for water?
- Why are camels so important for people who live in hot deserts?

Answers to activities

1 a Pupils should draw a diagram of either of the photos B or C on page 23 of the pupil book.

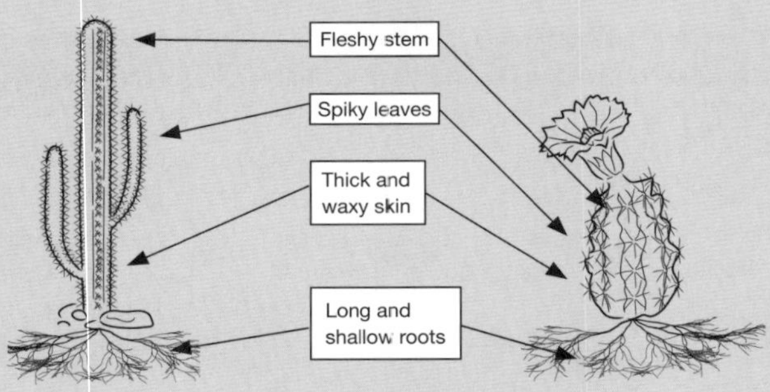

b **Fleshy stem** stores water in the stem for the cactus to use during a long period of drought.

Spiky leaves reduce the loss of moisture.

Thick and waxy skin reflects some of the sun's heat and reduces the loss of moisture.

Long and shallow roots soak up as much water as possible after rainfall.

2 Pupils should draw a diagram of photos D on page 23 of the pupil book.

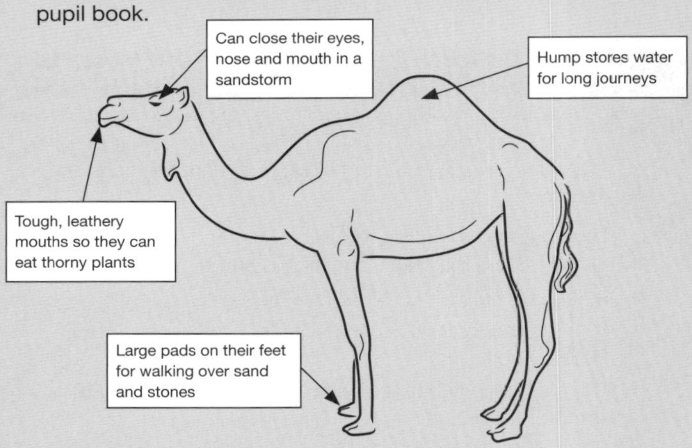

3 Use a camel because it can cross the desert easily. Camels have adapted to living in the desert and can survive without water for a long time.

Wear loose fitting clothing to allow air to circulate around the body because it is so hot. Wear something to cover the head so there is protection against sunstroke.

Carry containers which hold as much water as possible and a supply of food in case you get lost.

Pupil Book pages 24–25

What are polar regions like?

About this spread

This spread covers the main features of the climate and vegetation of polar regions. The difference between tundra and an ice cap is explained. The location of the polar regions is described and reference is made to the wildlife and vegetation that inhabit these areas. The effect of global climate change on the ecosystems of polar regions is considered.

Learning outcomes

By the end of this spread pupils should be able to:

- describe and explain the main features of a polar climate
- recognise the two types of polar regions
- explain how wildlife and the vegetation is adapted to polar conditions
- describe the threats to the polar regions of global climate change.

Key vocabulary

- **polar climate**
- **tundra climate**
- **ice cap**

Learning objectives

On this spread pupils should learn:

- about the main features of a polar climate
- that not all polar regions are the same
- that the vegetation and wildlife of the polar regions are unique
- that the polar regions are being affected by global climate change.

Skills builder

There is an opportunity to develop pupils' values and to consider the attitudes of those that are interested in the environmental threat to the polar regions. This could involve a role play to develop their verbal reasoning through putting forward a reasoned point of view. Producing a piece of analytical writing such as a newspaper article would lend itself to effective use of ICT through internet research. Software such as PowerPoint or Publisher could be used for presentation.

Further discussion suggestions

- Why are people that live in low-lying coastal areas in eastern England concerned about the effect of global climate change on the polar regions?
- Is the fate of the polar bear important?
- Why do polar areas have 24 hours of daylight in summer and 24 hours of night in winter?

Answers to activities

1 Polar climates have **short** summers, **long** winters and some **snow** throughout the year.

2 a i The temperature is –25 °C in January; the temperature is 5 °C in July.

ii The total precipitation in a year is 67 mm.

3 a **Tundra climate**: Northern Alaska and Canada. Northern Russia.

Ice cap climate: Greenland and Antarctica.

b The tundra vegetation is made up of low specialized plants that can survive a very short growing season.

c There is very little precipitation in the polar regions because the air is so cold that it cannot pick up much moisture. The drier the air, the less chance there is of precipitation.

4 The polar ice is getting smaller because the ice is melting. This means that the area that the polar bear can roam over when looking for food is getting smaller because where there was once solid ice, there is now water.

Pupil Book pages 26–27

Environmental regions enquiry

About this spread

The ecosystems enquiry could be used after pupils have completed the work on different climates and vegetation, or at the end of the ecosystems unit. It is one of five enquiries in the pupil book, and provides an opportunity to assess pupils' progress.

Learning objectives

On this spread pupils should learn:

- how climate affects the pattern of ecosystems.

Learning outcomes

By the end of this spread pupils should be able to:

- complete a table of climate information for different locations
- decide which type of ecosystem matches the different locations based on climate information
- draw a map to show the distribution of different ecosystems
- suggest reasons for the changes in vegetation from the north to the south of the continent.

What is the ecosystems enquiry about?

In this enquiry, pupils are reminded that in a natural environment climate is the main factor affecting the amount and type of vegetation. Different types of climate support different types of vegetation. In this enquiry, pupils have to decide where a range of different ecosystems are likely to be located on an imaginary continent.

In the enquiry, pupils:

- complete a copy of a table of climate information
- decide which ecosystem matches the locations in the table
- complete a map to show the distribution of the ecosystems
- draw diagrams to show the types of vegetation found from the north to the south of the continent, and suggest reasons for the differences in vegetation.

How can enquiries help with assessment?

For each enquiry in *Interactions* there is a checklist in the appendices. The checklist provides pupils with success criteria so that they know what is expected in order to produce high-quality answers and improve in the future. The checklist can be used in two ways.

- Pupils can use these as they go along, to check that they are meeting the success criteria for the enquiry.
- They can be used for assessment, either by you, as the teacher, or another pupil (for peer marking). Any element that is not ticked provides evidence that the pupil has not met all of the criteria.

Differentiation suggestions

For lower-ability pupils

Work with pupils to make sure they are clear about the steps they need to go through in order to complete the enquiry.

- You could provide pupils with copies of table A, map B and arrow C for them to complete. You could also provide them with simple drawings to go with arrow C and ask pupils to stick them next to the arrow at the appropriate point.
- It might be helpful to complete a couple of rows in table A so that pupils have fewer decisions to make about which ecosystems are found at different locations.
- For Activity 4b, you could explain to pupils that their reasons should mention latitude, temperature and rainfall.

For higher-ability pupils

Ask pupils to find climate graphs for some of the ecosystems shown in diagram G. They could stick these next to their drawings in Activity 4. They could also find out more about the vegetation in some of the ecosystems (or at least use the information on pages 14–15 on tropical rainforests and pages 18–19 on Mediterranean vegetation) and describe how the vegetation has adapted to the climate.

Erratum

Please note that diagram D on page 27 in the pupil book is incorrect. The diagram should be as below. This will be needed for pupils to complete Activity 1b.

D January temperature (°C)

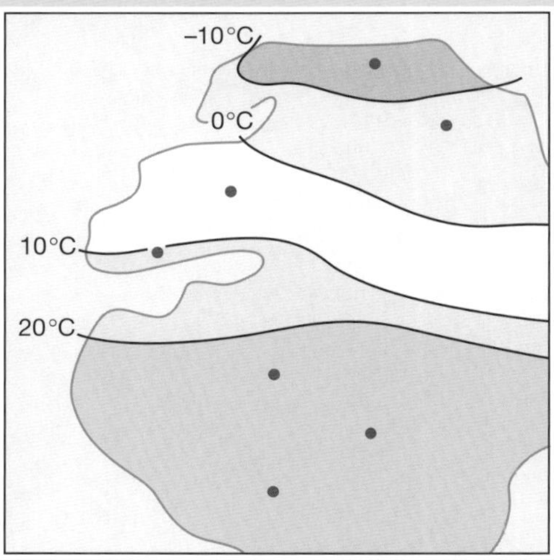

Pupil Book pages 30–31

Where do volcanoes and earthquakes happen?

About this spread

This spread looks at the location of earthquakes and volcanoes. Volcanic eruptions do not just happen anywhere on the earth's surface – they are confined to narrow belts or are grouped together. Earthquakes are happening all the time and can occur anywhere but, like volcanoes, most are found in long narrow belts. This spread includes two maps showing the distribution of volcanoes and earthquakes so that pupils can see how similar they are. The link with plate boundaries is investigated on the following spread.

Learning outcomes

By the end of this spread pupils should be able to:

- describe the distribution of earthquakes and volcanoes
- describe the location of the main zones of volcanic and earthquake activity
- use the internet to find out about an earthquake or volcanic eruption.

Key vocabulary

- **volcano**
- **Ring of Fire**
- **earthquake**
- **seismograph**
- **tsunami**
- **zones of activity**

Learning objectives

On this spread pupils should learn:

- that volcanoes and earthquakes occur in narrow belts (or zones of activity)
- that volcanoes and earthquakes often occur in the same places.

Skills builder

In geography a key skill pupils need to develop is the ability to extract information from a range of sources such as tables, graphs, diagrams, photos, newspaper reports, websites, and so on. Activity 7 provides pupils with practice in searching for websites and extracting relevant information. This is a skill that pupils need, not only at Key Stage 3, but throughout their study of geography.

Further discussion suggestions

- Why are volcanic eruptions easier to predict than earthquakes?
- What is a volcanic hot spot?
- What is liquefaction?
- Why did liquefaction make the 2011 earthquake in Christchurch, New Zealand so catastrophic?

Pupil Book pages 30–31

Where do volcanoes and earthquakes happen? *(continued)*

Answers to activities

1 a In narrow belts; In Iceland; In Japan; along the west coast of North and South America.

b Pupils are asked to name two other places where volcanoes may be found. These include:

- Indonesia
- the Philippines
- New Zealand
- Italy
- Hawaii.

2 The 'Ring of Fire' is named after the long narrow belt of volcanoes that runs around the edge of the Pacific Ocean. The word 'fire' is used because of the fiery nature of volcanic eruptions.

3

Volcano	Country
Fuji	Japan
Krakatoa	Indonesia
Ngauruhoe	New Zealand
Mauna Loa	USA
Mt St Helens	USA
Popocatapetl	Mexico
Paricutin	Mexico
Nevada del Ruiz	Colombia
Cotopaxi	Ecuador
Aconcagua	Argentina
Eyjafjallajökull	Iceland
Vesuvius	Italy
Etna	Italy

4 Earthquakes mostly occur in long narrow belts. There are two major belts:

- one that runs down the middle of the Atlantic Ocean
- one that runs down the West coast of North and South America and then goes round the western edge of the Pacific Ocean.

Other belts include:

- one that runs through the Mediterranean Sea
- one that runs through the Indian Ocean
- one that encircles the Caribbean Sea.

5 Possible answers include: locations on the Pacific 'Ring of Fire'; Iceland; Italy.

6 Possible answers include: North America (other than the Pacific Rim); Australia; Greenland; the UK; much of mainland Europe; large areas of Africa; and central and western Asia.

7 Pupils answers will vary. Make sure that they include all that is asked for in the question – a location map and a description of the earthquake, as well as causes and effects making use of labelled drawings and photos.

For example, Haiti earthquake 2010.

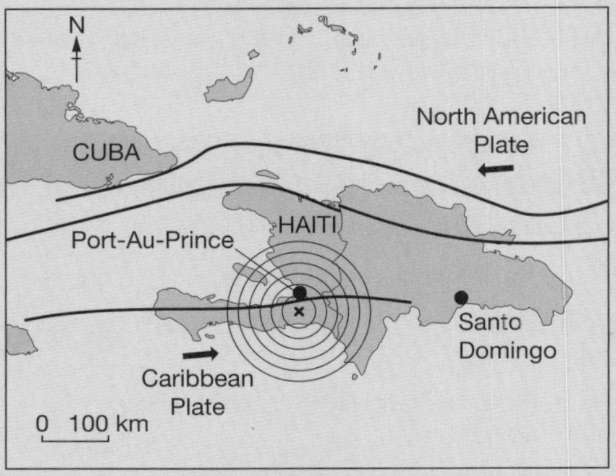

- The earthquake was caused by a sudden slippage along a crack in the earth's crust in the Caribbean country of Haiti.
- About 230,000 people were killed; 1.5 million people lost their homes; 180,000 houses were destroyed.

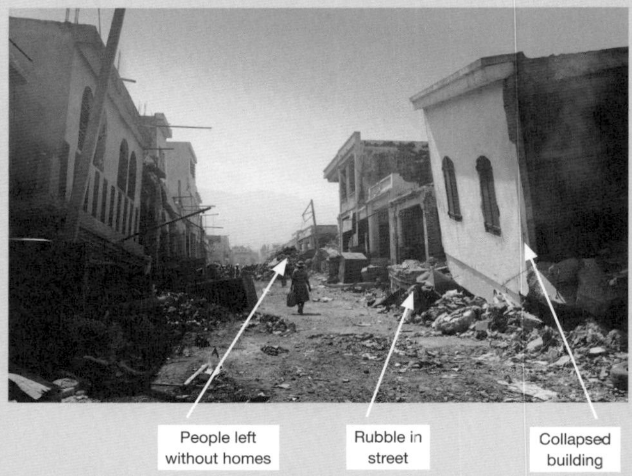

Pupil Book pages 32–33

How do volcanoes and earthquakes happen?

About this spread

This spread investigates the mechanics of how earthquakes and volcanic eruptions happen. It looks at the structure of the earth – the core, mantle and crust – and how the earth's crust is broken into huge slabs called plates. Plates move slowly and meet at plate boundaries. It is the movement of plates at plate boundaries that causes earthquakes and volcanic eruptions to occur. The spread includes a diagram showing what happens on the west coast of South America where the Nazca Plate is forced towards, and under, the South American Plate.

Learning outcomes

By the end of this spread pupils should be able to:

- understand that the earth's surface is made up of plates that move very slowly
- describe how volcanic eruptions happen at plate boundaries
- explain how the movement of plates causes earthquakes
- draw a diagram to show what happens where the Nazca Plate meets the South American Plate.

Key vocabulary

- **crust**
- **mantle**
- **core**
- **plates**
- **plate boundary**
- **magma**

Learning objectives

On this spread pupils should learn:

- about the structure of the earth
- that earthquakes and volcanic eruptions occur at plate boundaries
- that the movement of plates causes earthquakes and volcanic eruptions.

Skills builder

On this spread pupils are provided with a simplified map of the major plate boundaries, which also shows the direction of plate movement. This map provides pupils with an opportunity to develop their skills of interpretation (in terms of what the map shows) and also comparison – pupils are asked to compare the map with those on pages 30–31 of the pupil book, which show where volcanoes are found and where earthquakes happen. Pupils should see that there is a clear pattern that most volcanoes and earthquakes happen along plate boundaries. If pupils continue to study geography at GCSE level, they will be expected to interpret maps showing different things, to look for patterns and explain them.

Further discussion suggestions

- What causes the movement of tectonic plates?
- If new crust is filling the gap where two plates are moving apart, why isn't the world getting bigger?
- How can an earthquake create a tsunami?

Answers to activities

1 a The Eurasian Plate.

b Britain does not have any active volcanoes or major earthquakes because it lies a long way from a major plate boundary.

c The North American Plate and the Pacific Plate.

d Earthquakes happen in San Francisco as it sits on a plate boundary where two plates are moving past each other.

2 The correct order is:

- Plates move towards each other
- Plates rub together
- Friction melts the rock
- Molten rock rises
- Volcanoes erupt on the surface

3 Where plates move, or scrape together, it can cause friction, which results in earthquakes.

4

How volcanoes and earthquakes happen

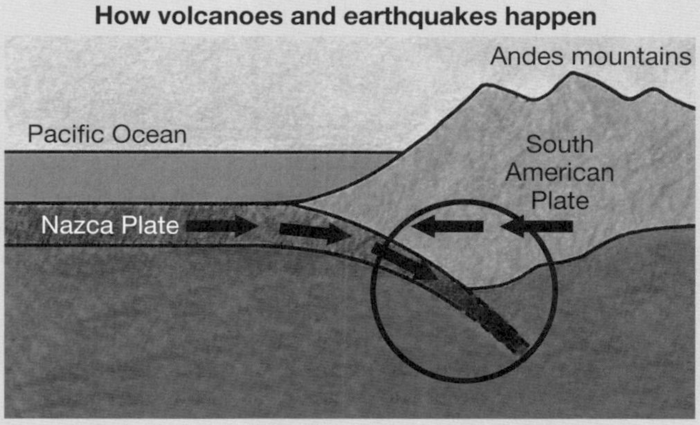

Pupil Book pages 34–35

What are volcanoes?

About this spread

This spread explains what volcanoes are, the main features of a volcano, how they might be active, dormant or extinct and how they erupt. It also includes diagrams that show the different types of volcanoes. To many pupils this is what geography is all about – massive explosions, great firework displays and new land being formed in front of their eyes – so build on this enthusiasm.

Skills builder

On this spread pupils have an opportunity to draw a sketch from a photo in Activity 3 and a diagram of a volcano in Activity 4. Drawing photo sketches and diagrams are key geographical skills. Pupils' sketches and diagrams do not need to be works of art, but they do need to be clear, show the key features and be labelled. Pupils will achieve higher marks at GCSE if they can draw clear, well-labelled diagrams.

Further discussion suggestions

- How does pyroclastic flow from certain types of volcano quickly devastate nearby areas following an eruption?
- Yellowstone National Park in the USA lies within a massive caldera. How was this formed?
- What are the three most abundant gases released by volcanoes into the atmosphere? What is their effect?

Learning objectives

On this spread pupils should learn:

- about the main features of a volcano
- what happens when a volcano erupts
- that there are different types of volcano.

Learning outcomes

By the end of this spread pupils should be able to:

- explain what volcanoes are
- describe the difference between active, dormant and extinct volcanoes
- draw a labelled photo sketch of a volcano
- draw a diagram to show the main features of a volcano and explain what happens when the volcano erupts.

Key vocabulary

- **volcano**
- **vent**
- **magma**
- **lava**
- **volcanic bombs**
- **ash**
- **dust**
- **crater**
- **active volcano**
- **dormant volcano**
- **extinct volcano**

Answers to activities

1 a Volcanoes are openings (vents) in the ground where magma (molten rock) from deep inside the earth forces its way to the surface.

b Active volcanoes are those that have erupted recently and are likely to erupt again.

Dormant volcanoes are those that have erupted in the past 2,000 years, but have not erupted recently.

Extinct volcanoes are those that are unlikely to erupt ever again.

2 Pupils are asked to give the meanings for the following words and can add sketches to make their explanations clearer and more interesting.

- Magma – molten rock found deep inside the earth.
- Vent – an opening in the earth's surface through which material is forced upwards during a volcanic eruption.
- Crater – a funnel-shaped hollow at the top of a volcanic cone.
- Lava – molten rock that flows from the crater of a volcano.
- Volcanic bombs – large lumps of molten rock thrown out by an erupting volcano.
- Volcanic cone – a secondary cone forms if the main vent is blocked and the magma is forced to the surface by another route.

3 **Sketch of Ngauruhoe, New Zealand**

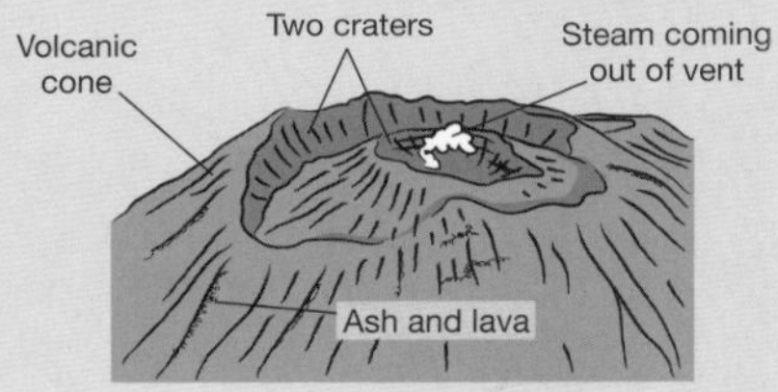

4 When a volcano erupts, the magma stored in the magma chamber deep inside the earth rises up the vent to the volcano's crater. It explodes into the air as ash, dust, steam, gas and volcanic bombs, or flows down the mountainside as a lava flow. If the vent is blocked, the magma is forced to find another route to the surface and forms a secondary cone.

The volcano is built up by layers of ash and lava from previous eruptions.

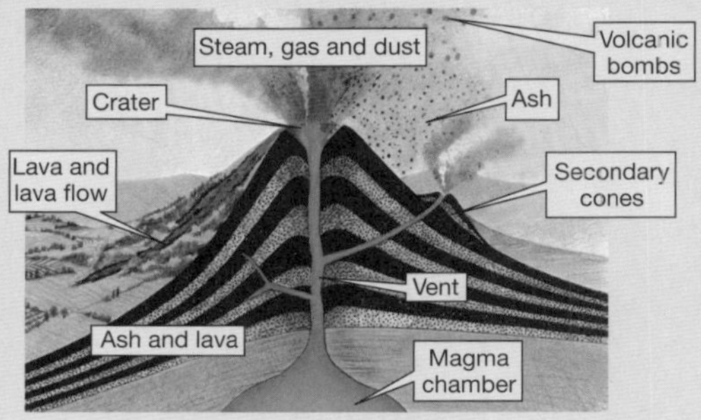

Pupil Book pages 36–37

What happens when a volcano erupts?

About this spread

This spread begins by introducing pupils to the idea of natural hazards (which include volcanic eruptions, earthquakes, floods and droughts, etc.) and explains why people want to live in volcanic areas despite the obvious danger. The spread then looks at Mount Etna, in Sicily and also Eyjafjallajökull in Iceland. Mount Etna was chosen because it is Europe's highest volcano and it is a name known by most people. The eruption of Eyjafjallajökull had an effect on many people throughout the world including disrupting air travel throughout Europe.

Learning outcomes

By the end of this spread pupils should be able to:

- explain the term 'natural hazard'
- describe what happens when a volcano erupts
- list the problems caused by an eruption such as those of Mount Etna and Eyjafjallajökull.

Key vocabulary

- **natural hazard**

Learning objectives

On this spread pupils should learn:

- that volcanic eruptions are a type of natural hazard
- what happens when a volcano erupts
- about some of the effects of a volcanic eruption.

Skills builder

Ask pupils to write a newspaper report on a recent volcanic eruption. They should describe the eruption, state when and where it happened, and describe some of the effects it had. They could include photos in their report. Provide pupils with suitable sources to use to find out the information they need, and give them a word limit.

Further discussion suggestions

- Which are the world's most active volcanoes? Where are they found?
- Mount Etna lies on a subduction zone between the African plate and the Eurasian plate. What does 'subduction' mean?

Answers to activities

1 Volcanic areas often have rich, fertile soil formed from the ash and lava from volcanic eruptions. These farming areas are attractive places to live, and so volcanic areas often have lots of people living in them.

2 a A natural hazard is a natural event that is a threat or danger to people and their way of life.

b Pupils are asked to name four natural hazards. Examples are volcanic eruptions, earthquakes, floods, drought, strong winds.

3 What happens when a volcano erupts?

Volcano gently rumbles and steams
↓
Loud explosion as volcano erupts
↓
Ash, bombs and lava blasted out of volcano
↓
Lava pours down the mountainside
↓
Buildings and property damaged
↓
Rescue service goes into action

Pupils can add simple drawings for each box to make their descriptions clearer and more interesting.

4 a

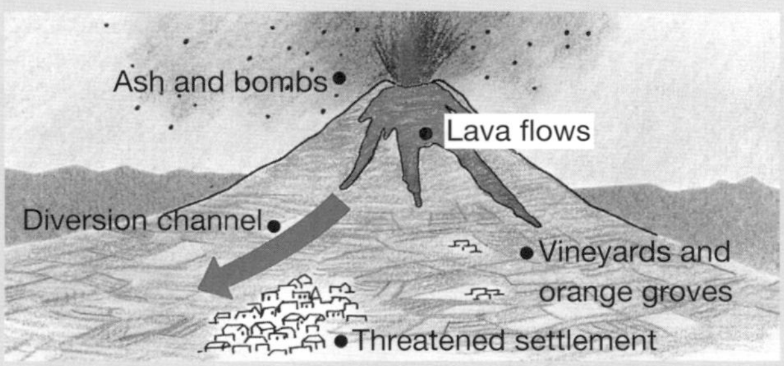

b Problems caused by Mount Etna erupting include the destruction of:

- three restaurants
- 25 houses
- a research observatory
- orange groves
- a hotel
- vineyards.

Pupil Book pages 38–39

What happens in an earthquake?

About this spread

In this spread the use of newspaper articles containing text, photographs and a map gives pupils an insight into the earthquake that hit Japan in 2011. Pupils are given details of both the immediate and projected long-term effects of the earthquake.

Learning objectives

On this spread pupils should learn:

- about the effects of an earthquake
- about responses to an earthquake.

Learning outcomes

By the end of the spread pupils should be able to:

- describe the short- and long-term effects of an earthquake
- prioritise the most effective responses to a natural disaster like an earthquake
- make use of some detailed case study information to illustrate a more generalised study of an earthquake.

Key vocabulary

- **epicentre**

Skills builder

This spread gives pupils practice in moving from a generalised to a more place specific exemplification. It will contribute to their sense of place and also allow them to develop their own value judgments. The newspaper articles provide information in two contrasting ways – text with a photograph and text with a map. This will help to develop pupils' skills in coping with a range of stimulus material, which will improve their ability to look for complementary and supplementary information from the differing sources.

Further discussion suggestions

- Would the responses to the earthquake be different if it had happened in a developing country rather than in a developed country like Japan?
- What is a tsunami?
- Which of the effects were caused directly by the earthquake itself and which were caused indirectly?
- Were the projections of the long-term effects proved correct? Use the website www.bbc.co.uk/news/world-asia-26524772 as a basis of discussion.

Answers to activities

1 Pupils' Fact File should include the following information:

Place: Japan

Date: Friday 11 March 2011

Time: 2.46 p.m.

Dead: 22,843 people + 2,667 still missing

Injured: many thousands

Homeless: 500,000

Damage cost: $235 billion

2 **Massive death toll** Early reports suggested that thousands of people have lost their lives, many thousands were missing and over a hundred thousand made homeless. We now know that there were 22,843 deaths with 2667 people still missing.

Major earthquake hits Japan On Friday 11 March 2011 at 2.46 p.m. an earthquake measuring 9.0 on the Richter scale hit the north-east coast of Japan. This was the fifth most powerful earthquake in the world since records began in 1900.

Tsunami horror The wave caused by the earthquake was nearly 40 metres high and some waves travelled 18,000 km. They travelled at 80 km per hour and reached over 10 km inland. Almost all communications in the area were put out of action.

Towns devastated The earthquake shook buildings and buckled roads while the resultant tsunami engulfed entire towns. Electricity supplies were cut off. Six million homes were without electricity and out of control fires blazed throughout the disaster area.

Transport links cut Almost all roads, railways, airports and port facilities were put out of action in the disaster area. This meant that getting survivors out was very difficult. Many roads were buckled by the earthquake and others were washed away by the tsunami.

Nuclear panic Following the disaster, a state of emergency was declared as two nuclear power stations were seriously damaged. There were two major explosions at the plants and major radiation leaks, resulting in the evacuation of many people from the danger areas.

3 The pupils' choices are less important than the reasons why they chose them. They should be able to recognise the short-term responses from the long-term ones, as these would be the most urgent. Any four except the first would be the best answers.

Pupil Book pages 40–41

What happened in the Indian Ocean earthquake?

About this spread

This spread builds on the previous one and allows the pupils to appreciate the more widespread effects of a single earthquake in one part of the world. It introduces the Richter scale for measuring earthquakes. The activities give further practice in measuring distance, this time on a small scale map as compared to the larger scale Ordnance Survey map extract used previously.

Learning objectives

On this spread pupils should learn:

- that the effects of an earthquake can be experienced over a very large area
- that an earthquake under the sea can cause a tsunami
- that the Richter scale is used for measuring earthquakes.

Learning outcomes

By the end of this spread pupils should be able to:

- measure distances accurately off a small scale map
- describe and explain the human and physical effects of the Indian ocean tsunami
- explain the relationship between the different levels of the Richter scale.

Key vocabulary

- **tsunami**
- **plate boundary**
- **Richter scale**

Skills builder

The annotated map gives pupils practice in interpreting a vast amount of diagrammatic and also textual detail. It will reinforce their understanding of timing and scale, as well as contributing to their sense of place. It will allow pupils to further appreciate how the responses to a natural disaster in developing countries, like those around the Indian Ocean, differ from those in a developed country, like Japan.

Further discussion suggestions

- In which countries shown on map B on page 40 are the effects of the tsunami likely to be the longest lasting?
- There are physical, human, economic and environmental effects of the tsunami. Which do you think are the most serious?
- Why would a bar graph be the best way of illustrating the figures in table A on page 40?

Answers to activities

1 **a** The earthquake happened off the coast of **Sumatra**.

b The five towns on map B affected by the tsunami were **Penang**, **Banda Aceh**, **Chennai**, **Galle** and **Male**.

c The town closest to the earthquake was **Banda Aceh**.

d The country with most deaths was **Indonesia**.

e The country with most people made homeless was **India**.

2 **a** 2 hours

b 3.5 hours

c Half an hour

3 **a** 200 km

b 1,700 km

c 2,500 km

4 **a** The Richter scale is a scale measuring the strength of an earthquake.

b The Gujarat earthquake was ten times more powerful than the 1989 San Francisco earthquake.

c The Indian Ocean earthquake was 100 times more powerful than the 1989 San Francisco earthquake.

5 Pupils' Indian Ocean Earthquake report should include the following information:

What happened? An earthquake beneath the Indian Ocean caused a tsunami.

Where did it happen? The earthquake was off the coast of Sumatra in Indonesia and the tsunami wave flowed westwards across the Indian Ocean.

When did it happen? 2004 (26 December)

What damage was done? The earthquake destroyed towns and villages in Sumatra and devastated coastal areas around the Indian Ocean in countries such as Thailand, Sri Lanka, India and the Maldives.

What were the effects of the people in the area? It is believed that over 283,000 people were killed or missing. Over 650,000 people were seriously injured and 1,700,000 lost their homes.

Pupil Book pages 42–43

How can the earthquake danger be reduced?

About this spread

This spread explains that many towns and cities in California have been built in the active earthquake zone along the San Andreas Fault. In order to attempt to reduce the worst effects of earthquakes, California uses a policy of prediction, protection and preparation for earthquakes. This spread looks at each of these in turn.

Learning outcomes

By the end of this spread pupils should be able to:

- understand that it is impossible to prevent earthquakes from happening
- draw a star diagram to show signs that suggest an earthquake might be about to happen
- explain how buildings can be protected from the effects of earthquakes
- draw a poster to show how people can prepare for earthquakes.

Key vocabulary

- **predict**
- **protect**
- **prepare**
- **seismograph**

Learning objectives

On this spread pupils should learn:

- about how the danger from earthquakes can be reduced by prediction, protection and preparation.

Skills builder

Pupils need to be able to understand the key terms used in geography. In the case of this spread, they include 'prediction', 'protection' and 'preparation'. These terms are used in connection with a range of natural hazards – from earthquakes and volcanic eruptions to hurricanes and flooding. Pupils need to understand the difference between these terms and be able to apply them to different examples.

Further discussion suggestions

- *'Drop, cover and hold on'* is advice given by official rescue organisations in the USA, and elsewhere, to people likely to be caught in an earthquake. What does this mean?
- Why should wall hangings and tall bookcases in your house be checked if you live in an earthquake zone?
- Why should you make sure you know the location of gas, water and electricity turn-off valves or switches if you live in an earthquake zone?

Answers to activities

1 a 'Predict' means that you can tell where and when something (in this case an earthquake) will happen.

b

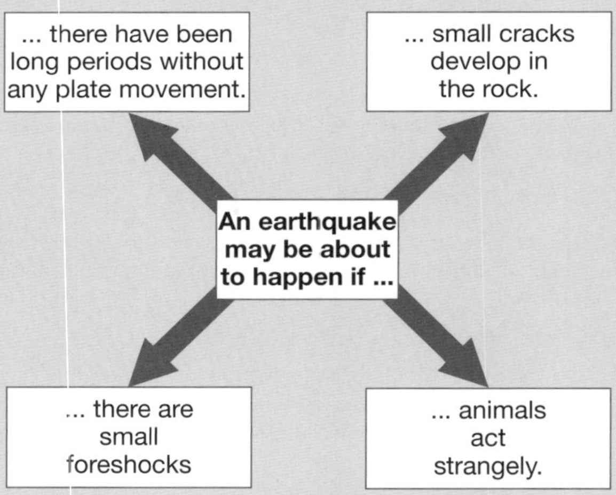

2 Hospitals and fire stations must ... not be built in earthquake zones.

Radio and TV stations should ... be prepared to give out earthquake advice.

There should be an emergency plan to ... help people who get injured.

Family emergency kits should ... include food, clothing, a radio and torch.

Architects and builders must ... follow the rules for safe buildings.

Every month, schools must ... practise what to do in an earthquake.

3 a People could be informed about earthquakes in different ways, including:

- practising earthquake drills in schools
- educating people, e.g. to turn off gas supplies
- setting up warning and information systems
- using radio and TV stations.

b Pupils' posters need to show what should be done in an earthquake and should include drawings.

Pupil Book pages 44–45

Two earthquakes compared

About this spread

This spread is a natural follow on to the work already covered on the Indian Ocean and Japan earthquakes. It shows how a developed country is better able to cope with the results of an earthquake, however severe, compared to one in a developing country. The differences in wealth help to explain why the three Ps – prediction, protection and preparation – are so much more effective in a rich, developed country.

Skills builder

This spread will build on earlier work on the factors leading to the difference in countries' level of development. Ask students to compare how their lives would differ if they lived in a developing country following a natural disaster like an earthquake. It gives an opportunity for descriptive writing which contributes to improving pupils' literary skills.

Further discussion suggestions

- Why might the cost of earthquake damage in a developed country be higher than in a developing country?
- Why would it take a less-developed country longer to recover than a developed country?
- What precautions could you take at school if you lived in an area which was prone to earthquakes?

Learning objectives

On this spread pupils should learn:

- that the wealth of a country is sometimes more significant than the strength of an earthquake in determining the severity of the effects
- that poor countries find it very difficult to deal with the effects of natural disasters such as earthquakes
- that the conditions in the country at the time of the earthquake and the ability to respond quickly after the disaster are very important.

Learning outcomes

By the end of this spread pupils should be able to:

- describe the difference in the responses to earthquakes in Japan compared with the less-developed countries around the Indian Ocean
- explain why less-developed countries usually experience more damage from an earthquake than developed countries
- explain the importance of the 'Three Ps' – prediction, protection and preparation.

Answers to activities

1 It is not possible to prevent all damage and loss in an earthquake because it is impossible to predict where or when an earthquake will strike or how powerful it will be.

2

	Japan 2011		Indian Ocean countries 2004	
	Good/Bad	*Reason*	*Good/Bad*	*Reason*
Effectiveness of the rescue terms	Good	Highly trained rescue teams reached the disaster area very quickly.	Bad	Local rescue workers were poorly prepared and arrived too late to save many lives.
Availability of transport	Good	Helicopters were used to transport rescuers and evacuate the injured.	Bad	Collapsed bridges and blocked roads hindered rescue teams.
Provision of medical facilities	Good	Hospitals were put on red-alert and saved many lives	Bad	Many people died of their injuries because of poor medical facilities.
Strength and quality of buildings	Good	Many building were earthquake proof and buildings in surrounding areas suffered little damage.	Bad	Badly designed and poorly built houses collapsed, crushing people inside.
Availability of money	Good	Over £100 billion was spent on repairing damage and preparing for the next earthquake.	Bad	Countries were too poor to provide the necessary protection.
Provision of aftercare	Good	People were familiar with earthquake drills and all new buildings have to be earthquake proof as far as possible.	Bad	Lack of food and unhealthy living conditions caused further deaths from starvation and disease.

3 **Prediction** Instruments for monitoring shock waves – the best way of predicting earthquakes – are very expensive, so less-developed countries can struggle to afford them. Developed countries can make greater use of them.

Protection Constructing earthquake-proof buildings is very expensive, as is the technological knowledge to build them. Both are in shorter supply in less-developed countries than in many developed countries.

Preparation The lack of hospitals and trained staff in less-developed countries means that they are less prepared to deal with earthquake casualties.

Pupil Book pages 46–47

The volcano enquiry

About this spread

The volcano enquiry can be used after pupils have completed the work on the eruptions of Mount Etna and Eyjafjallajökull on pages 36–37 of the pupil book, or can be used at the end of the volcanoes and earthquake unit. It is one of five enquiries in the pupil book and provides an opportunity to assess pupils' progress.

Learning outcomes

By the end of this spread pupils should be able to:

- use a map and table to identify routes to divert lava from an eruption on Mount Etna
- complete an evacuation plan for people living near Mount Etna.

How can enquiries help with assessment?

For each enquiry in *Interactions* there is a checklist in the appendices. The checklist provides pupils with success criteria so that they know what is expected in order to produce high-quality answers and improve in the future. The checklist can be used in two ways.

- Pupils can use these as they go along, to check that they are meeting the success criteria for the enquiry.
- They can be used for assessment, either by you, as the teacher, or another pupil (for peer marking). Any element that is not ticked provides evidence that the pupil has not met all the criteria.

Learning objectives

On this spread pupils should learn:

- how the damaging effects of a volcanic eruption can be reduced.

What is the volcano enquiry about?

In this enquiry, pupils imagine that they are a member of an eruption emergency team based in Catania, close to Mount Etna. The volcano has erupted and a huge lava flow is threatening the surrounding area. Pupils have to decide what action to take. They need to decide which way to divert the lava so that it causes least danger and damage. Then they must complete an evacuation plan for the people who are in most danger from the eruption. In the enquiry, pupils:

- complete a table showing some of the factors that need to be considered when choosing the best route for the lava
- decide which route to use, and describe its advantages and disadvantages
- complete an evacuation plan to move people away from the danger zone.

Differentiation suggestions

For lower-ability pupils

Work with pupils to make sure they are clear about the steps they need to go through in order to complete the enquiry.

- You could provide pupils with a partially completed copy of table D.
- For Activity 3, explain to pupils what the word 'evacuate' means.
- Provide pupils with a writing frame for them to complete the evacuation plan.
- You could also provide them with words to choose from for each question for the evacuation plan.

For higher-ability pupils

Ask higher-ability pupils to give reasons for their responses to the questions in the evacuation plan, i.e. they should explain their choice of who should be evacuated first etc. You could also ask pupils to find out about recent eruptions of Mount Etna and what action might have been taken to reduce the effects of the eruption.

Pupil Book pages 50–51

Why are we concerned about the environment?

About this spread

The environment provides us with natural resources. We consume these resources until they are used up, or use them in a way that may pollute the environment and kill its wildlife. It is important, therefore, that we conserve these resources and try to protect the environment for future use and limit damage to the environment – sustainable development.

This can only be achieved through careful planning and management. Planning may mean making decisions where there is a conflict of interest. The decision to represent the concern about the environment as a game of snakes and ladders is a deliberate one. The snake suggests a downhill path to a polluted environment, and the ladder the uphill path to a protected, improved environment.

Learning outcomes

By the end of this spread pupils should be able to:

- understand that if resources are misused, they can be used up or cause pollution
- understand that sustainable development means protecting resources for future use and limiting damage to the environment
- record how they use resources and contribute to environmental pollution and conservation.

Key vocabulary

- **environment**
- **resources**
- **pollution**
- **conservation**
- **sustainable development**

Learning objectives

On this spread pupils should learn:

- that if the environment and resources are misused, then the environment can be damaged
- that conservation of resources requires careful planning and management.

Skills builder

Activities 2 and 3 on page 51 involve pupils in identifying resources they have used, pollution they have caused and how they could conserve and protect the environment. This personal and practical experience will help to raise pupils' awareness of environmental issues. This will deepen their understanding of how the environment can be misused and why we should be concerned about it. It will enhance their understanding of how geography has meaning and relevance to their own lives.

Further discussion suggestions

- How green is your school?
- What can be done in school to show that it is concerned about the environment?
- Should economic gain, which provides money and jobs, ever be more important than concerns about its effect on the environment?

Answers to activities

1 **a** and **b** (examples are in *italics*)

The **environment** is the natural surroundings where people and animals live. *It is the combination of the physical (natural) environment of climate, landforms, soil and vegetation, and the human environment, which includes settlements and economic activities.*

Resources are natural materials which are useful to people. *Resources include things like coal, iron ore, clean water, soil, trees, mountains, wildlife and sandy beaches.*

Pollution happens when people harm and destroy the environment. *Rivers and the air can become polluted when resources are misused.*

Conservation is when people use resources carefully and protect the environment. *Things like the sea, the countryside, energy and wildlife can all be conserved.*

Planning and management is when people use resources without spoiling the environment. *Planning and management involves making decisions about things such as how and where we can build houses, create jobs and develop leisure activities while at the same time protecting the environment.*

2 Pupils should complete a table to show the resources they used, pollution they caused and how they tried to conserve the environment. They should use the table on page 51 of the pupil book as a starting point. Pupils' tables will vary depending on their individual activities.

3 Pupils will need to decide what criteria to use when assessing if their efforts have been successful or not.

Finance is likely to be the main consideration, either in strategies for preserving the environment or the possible economic loss in money and jobs caused by restricting activities that may damage the environment.

Pupil Book pages 52–53

Who cares for the environment?

About this spread

This spread explains that, while it is the government's job to try to protect the countryside, in reality there is a wide range of voluntary organisations that work to protect the environment. Many of the organisations concentrate on one aspect of the environment, e.g. the countryside, wildlife habitats or historic sites and buildings.

Learning objectives

On this spread pupils should learn:

- that government agencies and voluntary groups are concerned about protecting the environment
- that different aspects of the environment are looked after by different groups.

Learning outcomes

By the end of this spread pupils should be able to:

- describe the different types of environment that need special protection
- identify the types of environment that are looked after by government bodies and those that are protected by voluntary conservation groups.

Key vocabulary

- **historic sites**

Skills builder

In geography, pupils need to be able to interpret a wide range of diagrams, graphs, and so on. Sketch C on page 53 gives pupils an opportunity to interpret a drawing that shows different environments that need protection. This is not just a simplistic exercise. Pupils need to think about the environments shown on the drawing and make the link between the environment, the government bodies and the voluntary groups who are most likely to look after them.

Further discussion suggestions

- How is pressure put on the environment by:
  a leisure activities
  b overfishing
  c road, rail and air transport
  d waste disposal?
- What does the Environment Agency do?

Answers to activities

1 **Attractive countryside** includes things like rivers, lakes, mountains, coasts and moors.

Wildlife habitats are the homes of plants and animals. They include woods, hedges and wetlands.

Historic sites are things like stately homes, castles, industrial museums and monuments.

2 Pupils' responses may vary for this activity, but the most likely choices are as follows.

a (6) Country park – Natural England
(7) Newly planted coniferous forest – Forestry Commission
(10) Nature reserve – Natural England

b (1) Rock crags – habitat for rare eagles – RSPB
(2) Mountains with lake – The National Trust
(3) Old mill with water wheel, now an industrial museum – English Heritage
(4) Oak woodland – Woodland Trust
(5) Good fishing river – Environment Agency
(8) Remains of old castle on attractive coast – The National Trust
(9) Stately home – English Heritage
(11) Wetland (marsh) for water birds – RSPB
(12) Dolphins – Greenpeace

3
- The road needs to take the easiest and cheapest route.
- It should avoid environmentally sensitive areas.
- A possible route would follow the line of the old canal and continue along the good fishing river. The gradients will be quite gentle, but avoid as much of the oak woodland and the country park as possible.
- The road up to the lake could cut through the newly planted coniferous forest – they are not particularly attractive areas and are often devoid of wildlife.

Pupil Book pages 54–55

Why does wildlife need protecting?

About this spread

This spread considers why wildlife needs protecting. Pupils could be encouraged to find out the names of endangered species for themselves. They will find out that it's not just the larger whales, rhinos and elephants that face extinction, but also birds, insects, fish and plants. Although the elephant has been used as an example here, pupils could research any endangered species that captures their imagination. The possibilities for wall displays, discussions and the development of values are considerable.

Learning outcomes

By the end of this spread pupils should be able to:

- explain why some species have become endangered
- give reasons why endangered species need protection.

Key vocabulary

- **extinct**
- **endangered species**

Learning objectives

On this spread pupils should learn:

- about why some species are endangered
- why elephants are at risk
- what has been done to protect elephants.

Skills builder

Endangered species, and the effects of such things as killing rhinos for their horns and elephants for their tusks, are things that pupils may feel strongly about. Working through this spread is likely to generate some good discussion and develop pupils' values and attitudes. You could develop the ideas in the section on page 54 of the pupil book on 'Elephants in Kenya – the problem' to talk about the economic value of elephants, i.e. are elephants worth more alive than they are dead?

Further discussion suggestions

- What is a Site of Special Scientific Interest (SSSI)?
- What is biodiversity and why is it important to the environment?
- Wildlife faces threats from a variety of sources, such as habitat destruction, pesticides, pollution and other human actions. How would you form a group to protect the wildlife in your area?

Answers to activities

1 a Endangered species are those that are under threat of extinction.

b Pupils are asked to give five reasons why some species have become endangered. The reasons given in table A on page 54 of the pupil book are as follows.

- Crocodile and alligator skin is used for shoes, handbags and belts.
- Leopard, cheetah and jaguar fur is used for clothes.
- Hawksbill turtles can no longer breed on beaches since these are full of tourists.
- Rhinos are killed for their horns. A dagger with a rhino horn handle costs £10,000.
- Blue butterflies are virtually extinct in the UK as their natural habitat has been destroyed.
- Whales and dolphins are killed for food or can get caught in fishing nets.
- Elephants are killed for their ivory (from tusks).

2 Pupils can design either a poster or a T-shirt to suggest why elephants should be protected.

3 Pupils' responses will vary depending on which species they choose, and the sources of information they use. Pupils could use the WWF website: www.wwf.org.uk. They should click on 'What we do' > 'Safeguarding the natural world' > 'Wildlife'. This has information on a range of species that WWF is working to protect.

Pupil Book pages 56–57

How can industry pollute the environment?

About this spread

This spread looks at how the environment can be damaged by industry. Industrial pollution threatens almost every corner of the planet – from the air above us, to the ground under our feet and the oceans that surround us. Preventing pollution is not always the priority for governments and industries around the world, but it creates problems that can have enormous costs.

Learning outcomes

By the end of this spread pupils should be able to:

- name different types of pollution caused by industry
- explain how education can help to reduce pollution
- explain why some industries do not want to spend money on reducing pollution
- understand that cleaning up the results of pollution is expensive, difficult and can take a long time.

Learning objectives

On this spread pupils should learn:

- about some of the causes and consequences of industrial pollution
- about some of the ways in which industrial pollution can be reduced.

Skills builder

The skill pupils will develop on this spread is the ability to make the link between what people do (human activity) and the impact it has on the environment. Pupils should be aware that we all share some of the responsibility for environmental pollution in terms of our own actions, the choices we make about what we buy, how we travel, and so on. In raising this awareness, pupils can consider their own values and attitudes towards environmental pollution.

Further discussion suggestions

- In what ways might the oil industry pollute the environment?
- What is a reclamation scheme? Is it possible for a reclamation scheme to restore a ruined environment to what it once was?
- Asbestos is still widely used in the construction industry in developing countries such as India, China and Brazil. What are its dangers?

Answers to activities

1 a Air pollution (smoke from chimneys and exhaust fumes); water pollution (pipe discharging waste into the water); visual pollution (unsightly industrial buildings, materials dumped by the side of buildings, waste heap); noise pollution (from lorry); smell (from waste heap).

b The types of pollution most damaging to plants and wildlife would be air and water pollution. Smoke from chimneys includes gases that cause acid rain, and that can kill trees and fish. Warm water and waste materials released into rivers can kill fish.

c Pupils' responses will vary, but they should give reasons for their answer.

2 Pupils answers will vary but should be along the following lines.

Air

a There is smoke coming from the chimneys of the power station and steam from the cooling towers.

b The smoke is caused by the burning of a fossil fuel like coal to produce electricity. The steam is created from the heating up of the water that is used for cooling.

c Either replace coal powered power stations with renewable energy production like wind or solar or fit filters to the chimneys which will take out the pollutants before they can get into the air.

Water

a Waste materials have escaped from factories into the water.

b There may have been an accidental or deliberate discharge of the waste into the water.

c Companies that allow waste to go into rivers and lakes could face heavy fines and checks made to make sure that there are no accidental discharges.

Visual

a An oil refinery takes up a large amount of land spoiling the landscape especially if it used to be open countryside.

b The refinery was built in order to provide jobs and to meet the demand for refined oil.

c Strict planning laws are needed requiring factories to be screened by trees or that they are built on land that has little detrimental visual effect.

Environmental

a There has been an explosion resulting in a combustible material catching fire, causing smoke and fumes to get into the atmosphere.

b A pipeline may have broken, spilling a material like oil.

c Ensure that all machinery and pipelines are inspected regularly.

3 a Education can help to reduce pollution because as more people become aware of the dangers of pollution and the problems it causes, greater pressure can be applied to industry and governments to prevent further pollution from happening.

b Industries may not want to spend money on trying to reduce pollution as it could mean a reduction in profits, or an increase in the price of their goods.

4 Cleaning up polluted environments is expensive and difficult. It would be better to prevent industries causing pollution in the first place than to try to sort out the problems caused later.

5 There should be minimum number of words on the poster. Cartoon B should provide the pupils with some ideas. The slogan will allow them to show they have understood the concepts covered in this spread.

Pupil Book pages 58–59

How can environments be damaged?

About this spread

This spread considers how the extraction of raw materials as a result of quarrying can bring both benefits and problems. Quarrying causes a number of environmental problems, which range from noise and dust to landscape destruction. It is possible to restore quarries when they close and this spread looks at how a quarry near Hadrian's Wall in Northumberland has been restored.

Learning objectives

On this spread pupils should learn:

- that quarrying can bring both benefits and problems
- that damaged environments can be restored.

Learning outcomes

By the end of this spread pupils should be able to:

- list the impacts quarrying has on the landscape, people and wildlife
- list the benefits that quarrying can bring
- describe how a disused quarry can be restored
- recognise that attempts to improve damaged landscapes can be successful, but can be expensive and take a long time.

Key vocabulary

- **primary industries**
- **raw materials**
- **quarry**
- **National Park**

Skills builder

This spread looks at the issue of environmental damage within the specific context of National Parks. The example of a restored quarry in the Northumberland National Park is used on page 59. By applying what pupils are learning about to real places and environments, they will learn that geography is not just about theory, but it is about real locations, places and issues.

Further discussion suggestions

- Is damage to the environment always irreversible? Give examples.
- Gravel extraction has led to the creation of the Cotswold Water Park (www.waterpark.com), where dozens of lakes fill former gravel pits. What leisure activities might be enjoyed here?

Answers to activities

1

Harmful effects of quarrying on:		
Landscape	**People**	**Wildlife**
Quarries are dirty and dangerous Buildings and spoil heaps look ugly	Noise blasting and heavy lorries Air pollution as a result of blasting and lorries Heavy lorries cause traffic congestion	Wildlife is frightened away by noise from blasting and lorries

2 Benefits that the quarry could bring to local families include: work and income; an improvement in local roads; a source of materials that are used locally; attracting other industries and work to the area.

3 Pupils' notices will vary, but they should mention the facts that there is deep water (which is dangerous), disused buildings (potentially unsafe) and piles of mined waste (which could be hazardous and unstable).

4 a Grass and trees have been planted on old mineral waste; a dangerous steep slope has been reduced by moving soil; the lake has been made shallow and cleared of rubbish; a toilet block, car park and picnic area have been created; the quarry has been screened from the road by mature trees.

b Grass and trees have been planted on old mineral waste; wet areas have been drained; the lake has been cleared of rubbish; a nature reserve may be created.

5 Pupils' responses will vary depending on the interests of individual family members.

Pupil Book pages 60–61

What non-renewable and renewable resources are there?

About this spread

This spread begins by defining the terms 'non-renewable resources' and 'renewable resources', and then applies these terms to types of energy. The description of each type of energy is kept deliberately simple at this stage. The term 'non-renewable' is applied to fossil fuels, which are relatively easy to use but cause a great deal of pollution. The term 'renewable' is applied to those forms of energy that are often more expensive to use and yet cause far less pollution.

Learning outcomes

By the end of this spread pupils should be able to:

- give examples of natural resources
- describe the differences between non-renewable and renewable energy resources
- classify energy resources as renewable or non-renewable.

Key vocabulary

- **resources**
- **natural resources**
- **physical resources**
- **non-renewable resources**
- **nuclear power (energy)**
- **renewable resources**
- **energy**
- **fossil fuels**
- **sustainable**

Learning objectives

On this spread pupils should learn:

- that energy resources can be divided into renewable and non-renewable resources.

Skills builder

There is the opportunity to introduce pupils to the idea of classification and the need to look for common elements among a list of different geographical phenomena – in this case non-renewable and renewable resources. There is ample opportunity for using ICT effectively to research the advantages and disadvantages of these different varieties of resource.

Further discussion suggestions

- People are being encouraged to use sustainable resources whenever possible. What exactly does 'sustainable' mean?
- Is hydrogen a possible energy source for the future?
- What makes solar energy less efficient in the UK than at the Equator?

Answers to activities

1 **a** A resource is any material or product that we find useful.

b Natural resources are those that we take from the environment.

c Examples of natural resources include: scenery; soils; water; and raw materials such as minerals and fuel.

2 Pupils are asked to write down three differences between non-renewable and renewable resources. Four are given here.

- Non-renewable resources can only be used once. Renewable resources can be used over and over again.
- Non-renewable resources will eventually run out. Renewable resources will never run out.
- Non-renewable resources are quite easy and cheap to use. Renewable resources tend to be more difficult and expensive to use.
- Non-renewable resources create a lot of pollution. Renewable resources cause little pollution.

3 **a** Wood is a non-renewable resource as a tree may die if all the branches are removed. If trees are not replaced, this source of energy will eventually run out.

b Wood can be described as a renewable resource if trees are planted to replace those that are cut down and used as fuel.

4

	Used for heating	Used to generate electricity	A fossil fuel	Renewable resource	Non-renewable resource
Oil	✓	✓	✓	✗	✓
Gas	✓	✓	✓	✗	✓
Coal	✓	✓	✓	✗	✓
Wood	✓	✗	✗	✓/✗	✓/✗
Wind	✗	✓	✗	✓	✗
Wave	✗	✓	✗	✓	✗
Sun	✗	✓	✗	✓	✗

Pupil Book pages 62–63

Electricity and the environment

About this spread

Energy, as has been described on pages 60–61 of the pupil book, is needed to produce electricity. Much of Britain's electricity comes from thermal power stations, which use coal, gas and oil. Diagram B on page 62 shows how different stages in the production of electricity can pollute the local and global environment.

These pages will also get pupils thinking about their own values and attitudes by considering the question:

Is it better to have cheap electricity at the expense of polluting the environment, or to protect the environment even if it means paying more for our electricity?

Learning outcomes

By the end of this spread pupils should be able to:

- understand that coal, oil and natural gas are the cheapest ways to produce electricity
- list the effects that a coal-fired power station has on the local and global environment
- decide whether it is more important to have cheaper electricity or to protect the environment.

Key vocabulary

- **thermal power**
- **acid rain**

Learning objectives

On this spread pupils should learn:

- about how the production of electricity affects the environment
- about how the pollution caused by the production of electricity can be reduced.

Skills builder

As mentioned in the 'About this spread' section, these pages will get pupils thinking about their own values and attitudes by considering the question: *Is it better to have cheap electricity at the expense of polluting the environment, or to protect the environment even if it means paying more for our electricity*?

Activity 4 should generate some good discussion. Pupils won't have made the choice between electricity suppliers themselves – comparing prices and green credentials – but perhaps their parents have. Pupils could be made aware that it is possible to use 'green electricity' suppliers, such as Ecotricity, whose mission is to change the way electricity is made and used in Britain.

Further discussion suggestions

- How is natural gas linked to the petrochemical industry? How would this industry react to proposals to close thermal power stations in favour of new forms of electricity generation?
- Why is Norway able to export most of its North Sea gas to the UK?
- How did the tsunami of 2011 affect Japan's nuclear power industry?

Answers to activities

1 a Local effects include: large amounts of waste left behind after coal is burned; buildings, chimneys and cooling towers look ugly; buildings, chimneys and cooling towers take up large amounts of land; warm water is released from cooling towers into local rivers, which can kill fish; pylons are unsightly; living too close to pylons can cause health problems.

b Wider effects include: burning fossil fuels produces harmful gases; gases released by burning fossil fuels can cause acid rain; gases released by burning fossil fuels can increase world temperatures (global warming).

2 Pupils' responses will vary, but they are likely to include some of the local effects mentioned in Activity 1a.

3 Pupils' responses will vary depending on their own personal views about wind farms.

4 Pupils' responses will vary, but they should give reasons for their answer.

Pupil Book pages 64–65

How can we conserve resources?

About this spread

This spread looks at the idea that using fewer resources, using them more efficiently and recycling them, will all help to conserve resources that are non-renewable, and lead to sustainable development – a way of improving people's quality of life without wasting resources or harming the environment. There is a strong focus on personal responsibility and provides opportunities for class discussion and individual reflection.

Learning outcomes

By the end of this spread pupils should be able to:

- understand how resources may be conserved by reducing consumption, increasing energy efficiency and recycling
- explain how sustainable development helps to protect natural resources for the future
- complete a personal checklist for conserving resources.

Key vocabulary

- **sustainable development**
- **recycling**

Learning objectives

On this spread pupils should learn:

- about the different ways in which resources can be conserved
- what sustainable development is.

Skills builder

This spread builds on pupils' personal and practical experience of using resources. It will enable them to extend and deepen their awareness of how resources can be conserved by looking at the issue from a personal point of view. The skill therefore lies in making the link between things that are happening in the wider world (the enormous use of resources – whether it is oil, iron ore, coal, and so on) and their own lives.

Further discussion suggestions

- The more developed a country is the more energy it needs. Why is this the case?
- What methods have been used by the UK government and local authorities to make people more aware of the need to conserve resources and use them more sustainably?

Answers to activities

1 Pupils' lists will vary, but they should give at least six ways in which they could help to conserve resources.

2 **a** 'Think global, act local' broadly means that we should consider big issues that affect the world as a whole, but be prepared to do something about it on a small scale. For example, as the world uses massive amounts of energy, we could all cut down on our own personal use.

b Following on from above, if everyone took a small action to reduce their use of resources, the global effects could be huge.

3

Reducing resource consumption	Increasing energy efficiency	Recycling
Glass-fibre insulation in the ceiling	Low-energy lights with automatic timers	Clothing recycled
Double-glazed windows	Thermostats on radiators to control temperatures	Waste material like paper, cans and plastics reused or recycled
Wall cavities filled with foam	Carpet on floor	
Paper used sparingly	Books, equipment and furniture handled with care	
Draught-proofing on door		
Door closed during lessons		
Electrical equipment switched off when not in use		

4 Pupils' responses will vary depending on your own classroom situation.

5 Pupils need to copy the checklist D. Their responses to parts a, b and c will vary. For part d, pupils should describe how their decisions might help to conserve resources.

Pupil Book pages 66–67

Why is soil an important resource?

About this spread

This spread looks at the formation of soil with an introduction to the concept of weathering. It considers the importance of soil and how its fertility is an important aspect of its ability to grow plants successfully. It shows that soil erosion can be caused by both physical and human factors.

Learning objectives

On this spread pupils should learn:

- how soil is formed
- the importance of weathering and humus production
- the causes of soil erosion.

Learning outcomes

By the end of this spread pupils should be able to:

- explain how weathering is important in the formation of soil
- recognise the length of time it takes to produce a depth of soil suitable for plant production
- describe and explain the physical and human causes of soil erosion.

Key vocabulary

- **weathering**
- **humus**
- **fertility**
- **soil erosion**
- **deforestation**

Skills builder

Try undertaking some simple soil experiments in the classroom or out in the field. Simple tests of soil pH value, weighing and drying soil to show the water content, working a sample between the fingers to how whether it is sand- or clay-based are all useful. It may be possible to dig a pit in the school grounds to show the different soil horizons. Pupils should be encouraged to describe different soils using colour, feel and visual appearance as prompts.

Further discussion suggestions

- What descriptive phrases could be used rather than writing that soil is fertile or infertile?
- What is the correct scientific name for the study of soil?
- How many farmers change their soil?

Answers to activities

1 **a** Soil is a thin layer on the surface of the earth made up of minerals, air, water and organic material.

b Soil is formed in two stages. Firstly, weathering breaks up solid rock into small pieces. Secondly, air and water is added to the loose material which allows small plants to grow. These eventually decay to form the humus soil layer.

c Soil is an important resource because without it nothing would grow.

2

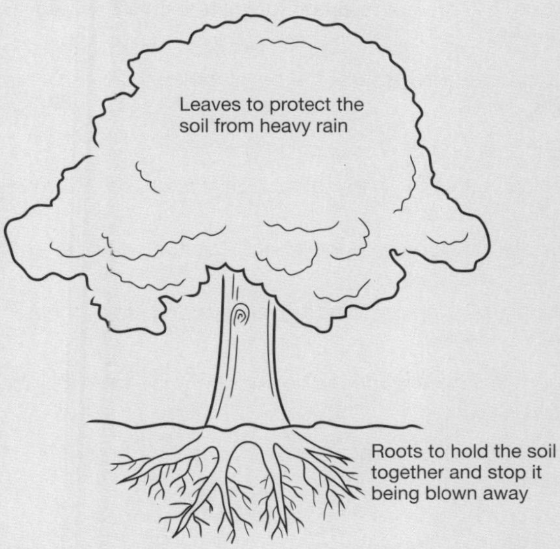

3 **Diagram 1** The trees have been cut down so that the soil is not protected from rain and is easily washed away.

Diagram 2 The farmer is ploughing up and down the slope and this allows water to run down the slope making it very easy for soil to be carried away, causing soil erosion.

Diagram 3 The farmer is keeping too many animals in the field. This means there is not enough time for the grass to grow back after it has been eaten. The grass therefore dies leaving the soil without any vegetation cover making it likely to be blown or washed away.

Diagram 4 The farmer is overcultivating the soil or growing the same crop in the field every year which reduces its fertility. It becomes very powdery and is easily blown away.

4 An example answer could be:

The effects of soil erosion

During a period of drought and wind	After a day of heavy rain
Soil loss from farmland Lakes fill up with eroded soil River choked with eroded soil Buildings covered with dust Roads blocked by blowing soil Land becomes a desert Dust storms	Soil loss from farmland Flash floods occur Lakes fill up with eroded soil River choked with eroded soil Landscape spoilt by gullies

5 Use the descriptions given in the answer to Activity 4 with appropriate protection measures: not cutting down trees/reforestation; ploughing across the slope; keeping fewer animals in a field; not growing the same crop year after year.

Pupil Book pages 68–69

Why is it important to protect our forests?

About this spread

This spread is concerned with the causes and effects of the deforestation of tropical rainforests and how this affects the native population in both positive and negative ways. The effects on the environment are described. There is an emphasis on the negative effects of deforestation, on both the local and global environment, although the arguments in favour of deforestation are also outlined.

Learning outcomes

By the end of this spread pupils should be able to:

- understand the role of the Brazilian government and international companies in causing deforestation of the tropical rainforests
- describe the negative and positive effects of deforestation on indigenous peoples
- describe and explain the effects of deforestation on the environment
- recognise that there are local and global effects of widespread deforestation.

Key vocabulary

- **forest**
- **slash and burn**
- **deforestation**
- **hydro-electricity**
- **ecosystem**
- **soil**
- **climate change**

Learning objectives

On this spread pupils should learn:

- that rainforests need to be carefully managed
- that deforestation is affecting the native population
- the causes and effects of deforestation.

Skills builder

This spread gives the opportunity for the development of pupils' own value judgments as well as an understanding of the attitudes and opinions of interested groups. These can be explored through descriptive writing, adding to the quality of the pupils' quality of written communication, or by verbal expression in a role play scenario. There is a great deal of statistical information on the deforestation of the rainforests available that could be the basis of some basic arithmetical manipulation and graphical representation.

Further discussion suggestions

- Why does the policing of the deforestation of the rainforests need international co-operation?
- Why should the Brazilian government not be allowed to do what it wants with its own resources?
- Do international companies like McDonald's have a responsibility to help the Brazilian Government rectify the effects of deforestation?

Answers to activities

1 a *Government polices*

- Roads are being built – trees have to be cut down to clear a way through the forest.
- People from poor areas in Brazil have been settled in forest clearings.
- Hydro-electric power stations have been built and this has resulted in the flooding of large areas of forest.

b *International companies*

- Forests are cleared to provide grazing for cattle. Much of their meat goes to fast food chains in USA and Europe.
- Trees are cut down for logs but only about 1 in 20 are suitable to be sold by international companies.
- Trees are cut down by international mining companies as they search for and mine iron ore, bauxite and gold.

2 a **Rainforest ecosystem** The trees that are not used for export are just burnt and many rare species like mahogany are becoming endangered. Wildlife habitats are destroyed with the loss of birds, butterflies, insects, reptiles and amphibians.

Rainforest soils When the trees are destroyed there is no humus to keep up the soil's fertility. The lack of trees means that the soil is easily washed or blown away.

Rainforest peoples People like the Amerindians have lost their traditional way of life of hunting and gathering and slash and burn. They are not resistant to western diseases and so are dying out.

3 The Kayapo tribe is **against** the development of the rainforest because:

- of the loss of their traditional way of life
- they cannot carry on using traditional methods of farming such as slash and burn
- they are at risk of western diseases as they have no resistance to them.

The Brazilian Government is **for** the development of the rainforest because:

- it will bring money into the country from the sale of timber
- it will provide jobs
- it will lead to the opening up of an isolated part of the country
- it will provide new land for farmers from poor areas of the country.

Pupil Book pages 70–71

The resources enquiry

About this spread

The environment enquiry could be done at different points in this unit. For example, it could be done after you have completed the work on why wildlife needs protecting on pages 54–55 of the pupil book, or you could leave it until the end of the unit. It is one of five enquiries in the pupil book and provides an opportunity to assess pupils' progress.

Learning outcomes

By the end of this spread pupils should be able to:

- assess whether different options for improving a nature reserve meet the given aims
- make decisions about the best ways to improve facilities within a nature reserve
- write a report providing details of the decisions made
- draw a poster to encourage people to visit the improved nature reserve.

How can enquiries help with assessment?

For each enquiry in *Interactions* there is a checklist in the appendices. The checklist provides pupils with success criteria so that they know what is expected in order to produce high-quality answers and improve in the future. The checklist can be used in two ways.

- Pupils can use these as they go along, to check that they are meeting the success criteria for the enquiry.
- They can be used for assessment, either by you, as the teacher, or another pupil (for peer marking). Any element that is not ticked provides evidence that the pupil has not met all the criteria.

Note that, before pupils begin their poster, they need to think about what makes a really good one. You could do this by showing pupils a range of posters – either those produced by pupils within school, or professionally produced posters. Once some decisions have been made about what makes a good poster, the most important characteristics can be added to the checklist.

Learning objectives

On this spread pupils should learn:

- about how planning and management can help to protect the environment.

What is the resources enquiry about?

In this enquiry, pupils are given the task of improving a small nature reserve. Their aims are to:

- improve facilities so that wildlife is protected and encouraged
- improve public access within the reserve
- improve visitor facilities and help promote enjoyment and understanding for the public.

Pupils are told they have a certain amount of money to spend and are given a range of suggestions for improving the nature reserve, along with their costs. Pupils should:

- work with a partner or in a small group
- complete a table to check whether the suggestions match the aims for the nature reserve
- calculate the costs involved
- write a report for the Project Director, which describes the decisions made and how the reserve will be improved
- draw a poster to encourage people to visit the improved nature reserve.

Differentiation suggestions

For lower-ability pupils

Work with pupils to make sure they are clear about the steps they need to go through in order to complete the enquiry.

Help pupils with their decision making (if necessary) in Section 2 by asking questions such as:

- Which suggestions are best for protecting and encouraging wildlife?
- Which suggestions are best for improving access to the reserve?
- Which areas of the reserve need improvements to the existing access?

For higher-ability pupils

Once pupils have completed Section 3 of the enquiry, you could ask them to peer assess another pupil's answer to this activity. Encourage pupils to set each other targets to develop their answers further.

Pupil Book pages 74–75

What are China's main physical features?

About this spread

This spread introduces a study of China by considering its main physical features. It shows that in a country the size of China there are great variations between one part of the country and another. It also gives another opportunity for pupils to gain familiarity with satellite photography and the use of false colours.

Learning outcomes

By the end of this spread pupils should be able to:

- describe the major differences in the relief, drainage, climate and vegetation between the north-west, south-west, north-east and south-east regions of China along with Sichuan province
- describe the main features of the River Yangtze
- extract detailed information from a climate graph and describe the pattern that it shows.

Key vocabulary

- **physical features**

Learning objectives

On this spread the pupils should learn:

- that there are great regional variations in the physical geography of China
- that these physical variations are of relief, drainage, climate and vegetation
- to describe the main features of an area's climate from a climate graph.

Skills builder

In addition to published satellite images, this spread gives pupils the opportunity to interpret the information on Google Earth. The use of a range of climate graphs will give them practice in recognising different patterns. This will involve taking an overview of the changes in the temperature and precipitation regime. They can illustrate this by referring to specific figures taken from the graph and noting any exceptions. Using a range of different graphs will help familiarise the importance of key words, 'compare' and 'contrast'.

Further discussion suggestions

- How does the physical geography of China change from the source to the mouth of the River Yangtze?

Answers to activities

1 Add the following labels to a copy of map B on page 75.

North-west

- *Relief* High mountains with inland drainage basins
- *Climate* Very cold winters and warm summers with a large range of temperature; rainfall throughout the year with 100 days of snow in winter; strong winds, especially in winter
- *Vegetation* Desert and semi-desert
- *Hazards* Extreme cold and strong winds giving wind chill in winter; dust storms and drought

North-east

- *Relief* North China Plain and the valley of the Huang He river
- *Climate* Very cold winters and warm summers with a large range of temperatures; rainfall throughout the year with 150 days of snow in winter; winters are dry but summers very wet
- *Vegetation* Forest near the coast with grassland further inland
- *Hazards* Extreme cold in winter, high humidity in summer; occasional drought; soil erosion and flooding

South-west

- *Relief* High mountains
- *Climate* Very cold winters and warm summers with a large range of temperature; nights can be very cold; wet summers and dry winters
- *Vegetation* Limited vegetation cover
- *Hazards* Extreme cold and strong winds giving wind chill in winter

South-east

- *Relief* Low-lying
- *Climate* Warm winters and very hot summers with a low range of temperature; wet summers and dry winters
- *Vegetation* Tropical rainforests
- *Hazards* Tropical storms and high humidity in summer

2 **a** south-east

b north-west

c south-east

d south-east

e north-west

3 **The River Yangtze**

The Yangtze is the **third** longest river in the world (after the Nile and the Amazon) and has the third largest discharge (after the Amazon and the Congo). It flows **6380** km from its source in **the Plateau of Tibet** to its mouth in the **East China Sea** (near the city of **Shanghai**). In its upper course it passes through deep **gorges** while in its lower course if flows over a wide **flood plain**. A large dam has been built to stop the **flooding** hazard and to improve transport and trade.

4 The likely changes are:

Physical narrow valley or gorge in a mountainous area, lake formed by Three Gorges Dam and a wide flood plain.

Human sparse population, isolated rural settlement, highly urbanized area.

Pupil Book pages 76–77

What are China's main population features?

About this spread

In this spread pupils will consider the wide variations in population densities in different parts of China and the factors that have led to either a sparse or a dense population. Details are given of the Government's one-child policy, which was introduced to cope with the problems of dealing with a large rapidly growing population. The advantages and disadvantages of this policy are considered along with the likely impact on China's future.

Learning outcomes

By the end of this spread pupils should be able to:

- describe the pattern of population distribution in China
- understand why there is such a difference in the population densities of the north-west and the south-east of China
- describe the main features of the one-child policy
- explain the disadvantages of the one-child policy.

Key vocabulary

- **population density**
- **one-child policy**
- **birth rate**
- **ageing population**
- **life expectancy**
- **population pyramid**

Learning objectives

On this spread pupils should learn:

- that there are wide variations in the population density in the different parts of China
- the positive and negative effects of a sparse or dense population
- about the one-child policy
- about future changes in China's population.

Skills builder

Population geography should not only cover consideration of absolute totals, but also the variations in the distribution of the population. Pupils will need to realise that both human and physical factors are important when trying to explain spatial variations. The opportunity could be given to develop pupils' cartographical skills by mapping population distribution. This will allow them to be introduced to and to appreciate the advantages of different forms of distribution maps in particular, choropleth and isopleth maps. Attitudes and values can be further developed by considering the rights and wrongs of the one-child policy.

Further discussion suggestions

- Why was it possible for China to introduce the one-child policy which was a very strict population strategy?
- Should the government be allowed to decree how many children a family can have?
- What are the main features of the predicted population structure of China in 2020?

Answers to activities

1 a A Beijing is the capital city and is China's political, cultural and economic centre. It is a major hub of the country's transport network.

B Shanghai is the main industrial city of China. It is a rich farming area because of the fertile soil in the valley of the River Yangtze.

C Hong Kong is an important trading centre. It is an important industrial area. This region has the warmest winters.

b D Very remote; it is mainly high mountains; it has a very severe climate because of the low temperatures.

E Very high mountains; it is very cold in winter; there is very limited farmland.

2 a The one-child policy was a government regulation that set a minimum age for marriage and couples were only allowed to have one child.

b China had a huge population and parts of the country were very densely populated. The population was continuing to rise at a very fast rate. The one-child policy was an attempt to slow down the rate of population increase.

c An example answer could be: It meant that there would be a better balance between the population and the available resources.

d An example answer could be: The government should not be allowed to tell people how many children they can have.

3 a There are fewer children being born and people are living longer into old age.

b Children will have to look after two parents and four grandparents.

Pupil Book pages 78–79

A journey through China

About this spread

This spread looks at a few of the huge range of attractions found in China and the reasons why an increasing number of tourists are visiting the country.

Skills builder

Pupils will be able to perfect their research skills from reference books and the internet, as well as to develop ways of identifying the key pieces of information rather than copying or downloading great 'chunks' of information. As a result of prioritising their information they will then be able to present it in a precise, pictorial form by creating a poster that shows readers the information in an easily understood manner.

Further discussion suggestions

- Which parts of China would be the best for you to visit if you going in the summer and which in the winter?
- Which parts of China should somebody go if interested in the history of the country?
- Which part of the country would attract visitors who wanted to look at dramatic scenery?

Learning objectives

On this spread pupils should learn:

- that China has a vast range of tourist attractions
- that some of these attractions are physical and some are human
- that to travel the country would take some time and require a range of different forms of transport.

Learning outcomes

By the end of the spread pupils should be able to:

- explain why China is attracting an increasing number of tourists
- describe the attractions of Hong Kong, the Chengdu and Sichuan provinces, the Yangtze river, Shanghai, Xi'an and Beijing.

Answers to activities

1 Answers will depend entirely on the student's own interests.

2

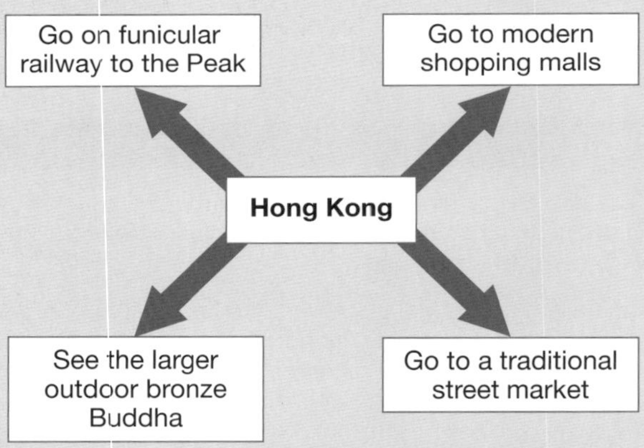

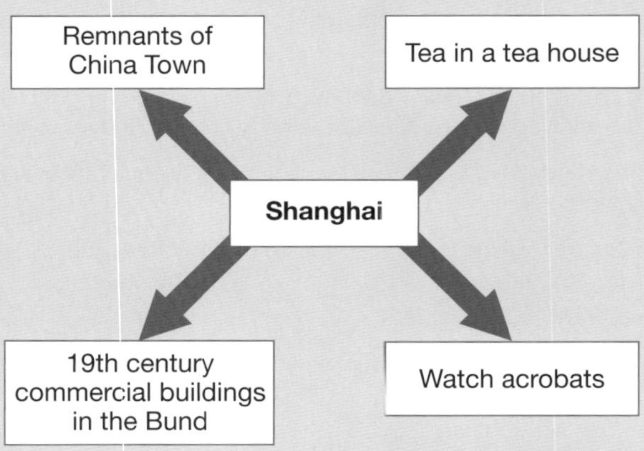

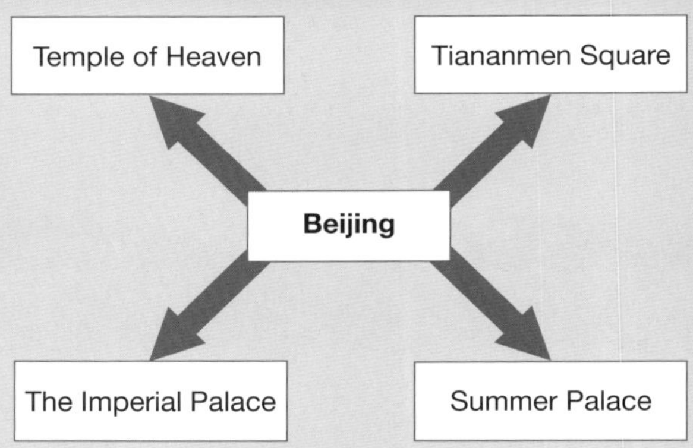

3 The poster should show evidence of research in addition to the information contained in this spread.

Pupil Book pages 80–81

What is it like living in Shanghai?

About this spread

This spread gives details of the changes that are taking place in China as it becomes a more urbanised society. The effect of movement from the countryside is shown to have increased the population of Shanghai. The growth of Shanghai has meant that the city has to cope with problems faced by urban areas worldwide, most noticeably traffic.

Learning objectives

On this spread the pupils should learn:

- how Shanghai has changed since the 1950s
- that Shanghai is facing many urban problems
- that a number of solutions have been tried to cope with these urban problems.

Learning outcomes

By the end of this spread pupils should be able to:

- describe how the buildings in Shanghai have changed as the city's population has increased
- explain why the population of Shanghai has increased to 23 million
- describe how building the new town of Pudong and improving communications has attempted to cope with the urban problems of Shanghai.

Key vocabulary

- **shikumen housing**
- **rural-to-urban migration**

Skills builder

The pupils are given the opportunity to use the table of information to look for overall trends and to come to conclusions based on evidence. The skill of analysing data and interpreting evidence is a fundamental part of geographical enquiry. Making good use of secondary data will help them when using primary data that they have collected themselves. There is also opportunity to illustrate numerical data through drawing accurate and appropriate graphical representations.

Further discussion suggestions

- How would the original inhabitants of Shanghai feel about its phenomenal modern growth?
- Are traffic and housing problems likely to be the only urban problems faced by Shanghai?
- What is the likely effect on the countryside of the rural-to-urban migration to Shanghai?

Answers to activities

1 a Shikumen were two- or three-storey buildings flanking narrow lanes or sometimes built around a central courtyard.

b The houses have electricity; people will be living near their friends and family so there is a good community spirit; waste is collected by carts that come around each morning.

c There is no running water; there is a great fire risk; the buildings are made of wood.

2 a In 1990 Pudong was an area of open fields where rice was grown.

b The river front has modern high-rise buildings and no open spaces.

c All the facilities are modern and there are shopping centres, restaurants, night clubs and plenty of opportunities for employment in the industries, many of which are hi-tech.

3 a The traffic was causing air pollution and congestion.

b There was a 47 km ring road built. It was followed by both a north–south and an east–west three lane motorway.

c *Advantages*

The traffic would be free-flowing and there would be fewer stoppages that cause air pollution and congestion.

It separated traffic from the housing areas.

Disadvantages

People were forced to leave their homes and had to move to new houses on the city outskirts – away from their work and amenities.

d A new international airport connects Shanghai with the rest of the world.

The number of tunnels has been increased so that more traffic runs underground. More road bridges have helped improve the flow of traffic.

Pupil Book pages 82–83

What is life like in rural Sichuan province?

About this spread

This spread emphasises that, despite the rapid growth of many of China's cities, the vast majority of Chinese people still live in rural areas, with many living as subsistence farmers. This gives the opportunity for pupils to compare the life in a traditional Chinese community with the very different one experienced by the inhabitants of Shanghai (pages 80–81). However, the growth of Shanghai and other cities means that there is an increasing demand for food to feed the city dwellers, which impacts on rural China. There is an increasing gap in wealth between the town and the countryside.

Learning outcomes

By the end of this spread pupils should be able to:

- describe the main features of the living arrangements in Sichuan province
- explain the difficulties of farming in rural China
- describe the impact of the rapid growth of cities like Shanghai.

Key vocabulary

- **subsistence farming**

Learning objectives

On this spread the pupils should learn:

- how people in rural China live and earn their living
- how rural China is changing
- the impact on the rural areas of the growth of cities in China.

Skills builder

This spread will give the opportunity for pupils to discover the impacts of change and the extent to which it affects both the built-up environment and the lives of the people. They will need to recognise that there are both internal and external forces contributing to change and they may have both negative and positive repercussions.

Further discussion suggestions

- Where would you prefer to live, in urban or rural China? Why?
- What types of people are more likely to leave the rural areas to live in Shanghai?
- Why do you think there is an increasing wealth gap between the rural and urban dwellers in China?

Answers to activities

1

	Old farm	New farm
Building materials	Wooden walls and doors	Brick
Number of rooms	One	Seven
Number of storeys	One	Two
Central courtyard	Yes	No
Windows	No glass in windows but iron bars for protection	Yes
Running water	No	Yes
Electricity	No	Yes
Sewerage	No	No

2 Recent changes in Hua Long. Pupils should use the headings in diagram G while referring to diagram E.

a *Shape of the village* It is built along a road.

b *State of the main road* The main road is modern with a bridge across the river.

c *Changes to shops* A friendship shop has been built which sells good quality goods at fixed prices.

d *Changes to public buildings* A bank and a village meeting hall has been built. There is a primary school funded by a charity organisation.

e *Improvements to the quality of life* There are better-built houses which are stronger and more hygienic.

Pupil Book pages 84–85

Shenzhen – a powerhouse in the Chinese economy

About this spread

This spread is concerned with the modern economic development of China using Shenzhen as an example, with particular reference to the five Special Economic Zones. The stages in the development of this industrial area are considered. The pupils should consider the growth of China as a global industrial power and investigate how rapid growth brings associated problems. Furthermore, parts of China, in particular the rural areas, have not gained much in the way of benefits from the industrial growth of the country.

Learning outcomes

By the end of the spread pupils should be able to:

- explain why industry developed in the Shenzhen Special Economic Zone
- describe the type of industrial growth that has taken place
- understand the concept of interdependence
- describe the problems associated with rapid economic growth on the environment the people and in the rural parts of China.

Key vocabulary

- **trade**
- **Special Economic Zones**
- **migrant workers**
- **emerging country**
- **interdependent**

Learning objectives

On this spread pupils should learn:

- that China has undergone great economic development
- that foreign companies have invested in China and helped the development of high-tech industries
- that there are problems associated with rapid economic development.

Skills builder

The opportunity could be taken to add a numeracy aspect to the study of China's economic growth by creating graphs of some of the country's industrial statistics which are readily available on the internet. If the statistics are available on the output of different types of industry, or from different parts of the country, then the use of proportional symbols could be introduced. Pictograms could work as a lower-ability alternative.

Further discussion suggestions

- Why would a UK company want to set up a factory in China?
- What examples do you have at home of articles made in China?
- What are the possible effects of the growth of industry in China on industries in the UK?

Answers to activities

1 a Shenzhen is situated between the Pearl River estuary and Dapeng Bay, about 20 km north of Hong Kong. It is connected by a main railway line to Beijing and Shanghai.

b In 1980, Shenzhen was a small settlement with a population of 20,000 people.

c Shenzhen is very built up, with a large number of high rise buildings and a modern dual-carriageway road system.

2 **Land values** These are much lower than in neighbouring Hong Kong.

Site Situated on a deep water harbour that is an ideal site for trading with the world.

Transport Situated on the main railway line to Beijing and Shanghai.

Government help The Chinese government set up Shenzhen as a Special Economic Zone.

Labour Workers' wages are much lower than in Hong Kong.

Finance Incentives were offered by the government to attract firms from abroad.

3 a There has been rapid growth in high-tech industries such as computer software, IT, mobile phones, medical and pharmaceutical industries, and biotechnology.

b It has provided work for large numbers of people, including the 6 million migrants who return home at weekends.

c The rural areas have not benefitted from China's economic growth. This is because they are losing people due to rural-to-urban migration. None of the proceeds have been invested in the rural areas and foreign companies have tended only to invest in the Special Economic Zones such as Shenzhen.

Pupil Book pages 86–87

The China enquiry

About this spread

The China enquiry can be used after the pupils have completed the work considering China as an emerging nation. It is one of five enquiries in the pupil book that can be used to assess pupils' progress.

Learning objectives

On this spread pupils should learn:

- there are different ways of measuring development
- the stage of development reached by China.

Learning outcomes

By the end of this spread pupils should be able to:

- understand the meaning of economic, social and cultural factors
- rank these factors according to their own value judgments
- use graphical representations of different measures of development
- come to a conclusion as to the level of development reached by China.

Key vocabulary

- **developed country**
- **developing country**
- **food supply**
- **literacy rate**

What is the enquiry about?

In this enquiry the pupils have to understand the meaning of different measures of development and to use their own opinion to put them in order of importance. They are required to come to a conclusion as to the stage of development reached by China, based on the evidence presented.

In the enquiry, pupils:

- define and explain the importance of specialist terms dealing with development measures
- do a diamond-ranking exercise to show their opinion of the measures they consider more or less important
- complete graphical representations of some statistical information related to development
- come to a conclusion as to the stage of development reached by China.

How can enquiries help with assessment?

For each enquiry in *Interactions* there is a checklist in the appendices. The checklist provides pupils with success criteria so that they know what is expected in order to produce high-quality answers and improve in the future. The checklist can be used in two ways.

- Pupils can use these as they go along, to check that they are meeting the success criteria for the enquiry.
- They can be used for assessment, either by you, as the teacher, or another pupil (for peer marking). Any element that is not ticked provides evidence that the pupil has not met all the criteria.

Differentiation suggestions

For lower-ability pupils

Work with the pupils to make sure they are clear about the steps they need to go through in order to complete the enquiry.

- For the definition activity, a heads and tails exercise could be used where the measure and its definition are given and they have to link them up.
- The pupils could be given partly completed bar graphs, in which the axes are already labelled and the scale indicated.
- Provide a writing frame where the headings, economic, social and cultural factors are given as headings and indicate that the pupils should add two pieces of information under each to show that China is still a developing country.
- Use a cloze exercise format for pupils to complete when writing their conclusion.

For higher-ability pupils

These pupils should be required to give their reasons for the conclusions they reach. Instead of merely drawing the bar graphs they should be required to describe and interpret them, and indicate any similarities and differences. Any exceptions to the general picture that emerges should be noted.

Opportunities could be given for these pupils to research other measures of development that may or may not support the conclusions reached based on the measures covered on the spread.

For example, look at the percentage of the population that has access to safe water or the number of tractors per 1000 population.

They could also be introduced to the Human Development Index (HDI) which, instead of using a single measure, combines literacy rate, life expectancy and infant mortality to give an indication of the population's quality of life rather than just measuring their standard of living.

Pupil Book pages 90–91

Where in the world ...?

About this spread

This spread consists of a large world map showing some of the world's most important rivers, mountain ranges, cities and oceans. This has been used to emphasise the global nature of world development and to confirm the importance of place as an element of geography learning. It also provides an opportunity for some good location geography. Pupils will be able to use atlases in connection with this spread, using the contents page and index, and latitude and longitude as a practical aid to finding places.

Learning objectives

On this spread pupils should learn:

- the location of some of the world's largest cities, longest rivers and highest mountains.

Learning outcomes

By the end of this spread pupils should be able to:

- use a world map and an atlas to locate places.

Skills builder

This spread, as already mentioned, provides a great opportunity for pupils to learn where in the world places are in a way that should be fun and engaging. It reminds pupils of the importance of learning about places in geography. The top ten of the world's largest cities will encourage pupils to learn their location and distribution, even if the population figures need updating. Encourage pupils to think about which countries those cities are located in. Are they richer or poorer countries? How many of them are richer or poorer? Why do they have such large populations?

Further discussion suggestions

- Where in the world is Scandinavia and which countries are found there?
- Where in the world are the Mediterranean Sea and the Red Sea?
- What is an 'isthmus', and where in the world is the Isthmus of Panama? Why was it considered important to construct a canal there?

Answers to activities

1 Pupils should be able to find the world's largest cities and longest rivers from the map and tables on pages 90–91.

2
1 Aconcagua
2 Kilimanjaro
3 Buenos Aires
4 Nile
5 Everest
6 Indian
7 Andes
8 Himalayas
9 Shanghai
10 Amazon
11 Rockies
12 Atlantic
13 Southern
14 Mississippi
15 New York
16 Moscow
17 Cairo

3 **Continent** Africa

Rivers Nile, Congo, Zambezi

Deserts Sahara, Kalahari

Highest mountain Kilimanjaro

Volcanoes Kilimanjaro

Main towns Cape Town, Johannesburg, Nairobi, Cairo, Lagos, Accra

Continent Asia

Rivers Huang Ho, Yangtze, Ganges, Ob

Deserts Gobi, Thar

Highest mountain Everest

Volcanoes Fuji, Krakatoa

Main towns Mumbai, Kolkata, Delhi, Beijing, Shanghai, Seoul, Tokyo, Kyoto, Singapore, Jakarta

Pupil Book pages 92–93

Too many people?

About this spread

This spread looks at population distribution and growth. This is a complex issue and these pages provide a simplified version of the effects of population, and overpopulation, on development. One of the paradoxes of population and development is that a lot of countries do have the resources they need for their people, e.g. some overpopulated countries grow enough food for everyone, but people are too poor to afford it. Many different approaches are used to try to reduce population problems and one way of slowing down population growth is through birth-control policies. China is used as an example of the one-child policy.

Learning outcomes

By the end of this spread pupils should be able to:

- describe the global distribution of areas with a high population density
- identify those areas where high population densities and rapid population growth are causing problems
- list some of the problems that can result from overpopulation in a country like India
- compare the reasons for the differences in population growth in India and China.

Key vocabulary

- **development**
- **living standards (standard of living)**
- **quality of life**
- **overpopulated**
- **population growth**
- **resources**
- **one-child families**
- **birth control**

Learning objectives

On this spread pupils should learn:

- what development means
- that overpopulation is one reason for some countries' lack of development
- that some countries try to limit population growth in order to help development and living standards.

Skills builder

Using maps is a key geographical skill. Pupils need to be able to identify patterns and describe distributions shown on maps. The map of world population distribution shown on page 92 and the text on this page enables pupils to see that some places in the world are very crowded while other places have very few people. Some crowded areas have high living standards and a good quality of life; some have rising living standards and an improving quality of life, while others have low living standards and a poor quality of life.

The map on page 92 is a choropleth map, which uses different colours or shading to show differences between places and distributions. Pupils can refer to pages 112–113 of *Nelson Key Geography Connections* if they need more help in understanding what choropleth maps show and how to create them.

Further discussion suggestions

- China is the country with the world's largest population. Which country has the second-largest population?
- Which nation is the most densely populated in the world?
- What is a megacity?

Answers to activities

1 Pupils' responses to this activity will vary, but the main points they should be thinking about are given below.

a The room would soon become too crowded to work in.

b There would be a shortage of desks, chairs, books, pens, paper, and so on.

c The quality of learning would go down. Pupils would receive less help and attention and would not receive such a good education.

2 a 'Overpopulation' is when there are more people living in an area than that area can support.

b Problems may include: a lowering of living standards; a poorer quality of life; a shortage of food.

3 a

	Rural India	China
Children needed to do work	✓	✗
Children needed for old age	✓	✗
Pension scheme for old age	✗	✓
Good health care	✗	✓
Disease problems	✓	✗
Large families	✓	✗
Improved conditions	✗	✓
Only slow improvement	✓	✗

4 The advantages of small families include: higher living standards; a better quality of life; an improvement in level of development.

5 Crowded places like the EU and eastern USA have high living standards and a good quality of life because:

- the population is only growing slowly or, in some places, actually declining
- the population is generally rich and has the money to pay for medical and welfare facilities
- older people get a pension when they stop working.

Pupil Book pages 94–95

How do jobs affect development?

About this spread

This spread looks at the link between development and employment structure. As countries develop, a typical pattern is for the labour force to move from primary occupations into manufacturing (secondary industries), followed by a move into services (tertiary industries). Map B on page 95 of the pupil book shows the variations in employment structure between different countries. The employment structure of a place therefore changes over time. Activity 4 on page 95 of the pupil book uses Britain as an example to show how this happens.

Learning outcomes

By the end of this spread pupils should be able to:

- understand the link between the employment structure of a country and its level of development
- identify the most and least developed countries based on employment structures
- draw pie charts to show how the employment structure in Britain has changed over time.

Key vocabulary

- **primary activities**
- **secondary activities**
- **tertiary activities**
- **employment structure**

Learning objectives

On this spread pupils should learn:

- that employment structure changes as countries develop
- that employment structures of countries change over time.

Skills builder

Activity 4 asks pupils to use employment data of Britain over different periods to draw three pie charts. Pupils need to be able to draw and interpret a range of different types of graphs and charts in geography. If they continue to study geography at GCSE level, they will be expected to construct and interpret a variety of graphs including line, bar, divided bar, scattergraphs and pie charts. Understanding how to draw and interpret these graphs at Key Stage 3 will stand them in good stead for their GCSE course.

Further discussion suggestions

- What primary industries are still important in the UK?
- What is quaternary industry?
- How does the employment structure of a NIC (Newly Industrialised Country) differ from that of a developing country?

Answers to activities

1 'Employment structure' is the proportion of the population working in primary, secondary and tertiary jobs.

2 The correct statements are:

- Employment structures vary from place to place.
- Employment structures change from time to time.
- Poor countries have many workers in primary industries.
- Rich countries have fewer workers in primary industries.

3 a The four most developed countries are USA, UK, Italy and Japan.

b The eight least developed countries are Mexico, Peru, Ghana, Nigeria, Kenya, Egypt, India and Bangladesh.

4 a and **b**

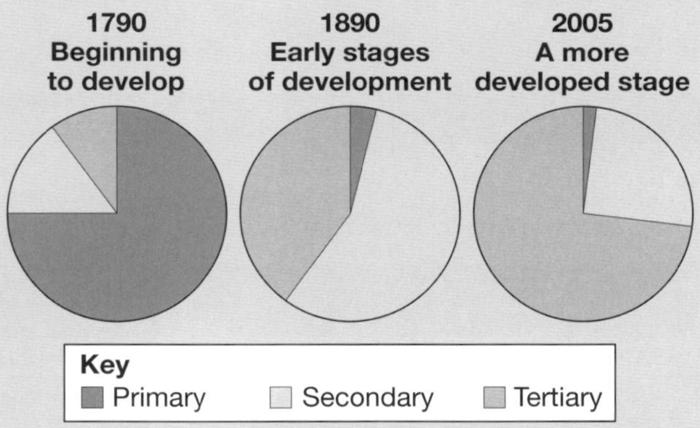

c As Britain developed from 1790 onwards, the proportion of jobs in primary industries fell. Initially, the number of jobs in secondary industries rose (from 1790 to 1890), but by 2005 the number of jobs in secondary industries had fallen as the number of jobs in tertiary industries rose.

5 The living standards in Bangladesh and Kenya are likely to be low for the majority of people because the country is poor. There is not enough money to provide modern buildings, welfare and medical facilities. In Italy and Japan there is a more developed educational system and so the majority of people have the necessary skills to get better paid jobs to enjoy a better standard of living.

Pupil Book pages 96–97

How does trade affect development?

About this spread

This spread looks at the inequalities of trade. Pupils need to know about the type and value of goods traded between richer and poorer countries. The main ideas that pupils need to understand are that:

- richer countries have a greater share of the world's income from exports than poorer countries
- poorer countries export more low-value primary goods while richer countries mainly export high-value manufactured goods
- many poorer countries rely heavily on just one major export, which can result in an unstable economy.

Learning outcomes

By the end of this spread pupils should be able to:

- understand that trade is important because it helps countries to share resources and earn money
- describe the differences between the nature and value of exports of richer and poorer countries
- explain why countries that depend on one export commodity can have problems.

Key vocabulary

- **trade**
- **exports**
- **imports**
- **primary goods**
- **manufactured goods**

Learning objectives

On this spread pupils should learn:

- about the nature of trade
- why richer countries earn more from trade than poorer countries
- about the problems of relying on one export commodity.

Skills builder

The activities on this spread require pupils to analyse and sort a range of data about selected countries. In Activity 1, pupils should:

- list countries in order of wealth
- sort exports as primary or manufactured goods
- identify countries that are less developed.

In Activity 3, they are asked to:

- identify countries that depend on one product for over three-quarters of their exports
- identify those countries that depend on one product for between half and three-quarters of their exports.

There will be many occasions in geography where pupils have to analyse data. They will need to use a range of techniques to organise the data and make sense of it.

Further discussion suggestions

- How can value be added to raw materials such as iron ore, cotton, flax or crude oil before export?
- Which will help countries develop quicker – trade or aid?
- What is OPEC, and what does it do?

Answers to activities

1 a, b, c and **d**

There are ten countries to place in the table.

Country	GNP (US$/person)	Primary exports	Manufactured exports
USA	49,965		Machinery, chemicals
Japan	46,720		Electrical goods, cars
UK	38,514		Machinery, chemicals
Italy	33,115		Machinery, clothing
Brazil	11,340	Coffee, meat	Machinery
China	6,091		Manufactured goods, clothing
Ghana	3,501	Cocoa, aluminium, timber	
Egypt	3,187	Oil, fruit, vegetables	
India	1,508		Machinery, chemical products
Kenya	862	Coffee, tea	

e More developed countries (USA, Japan, UK and Italy) export mainly manufactured products. Less-developed countries largely export primary products – Brazil has the highest GDP of the less-developed countries, and exports a mix of primary and manufactured products. As a country develops, such as India, it will export more manufactured products.

2

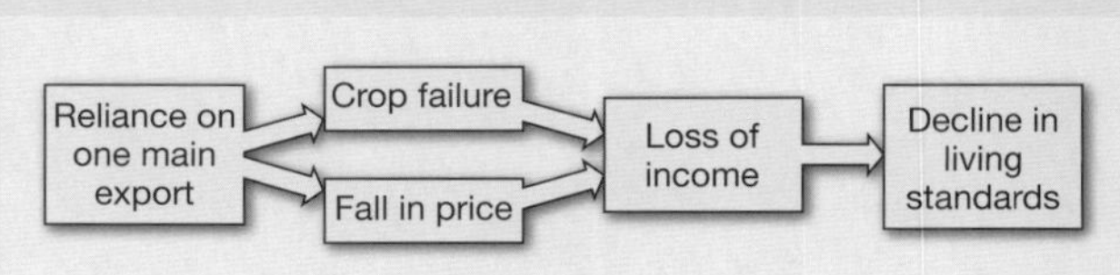

3 a Zambia, Nigeria, Cuba, Laos and Ghana depend on one product for over three-quarters of their exports. Bangladesh, Egypt and Botswana depend on one product for between half and three-quarters of their exports.

b Countries that depend mainly on one export often have money problems because if the crop fails, they have no other exports to replace the income. Alternatively, if the price on the world market falls, their income will fall.

Pupil Book pages 98–99

Is development spread evenly?

About this spread

This spread begins by reminding pupils that development is about progress and making life better for people. It then goes on to look at how development can be measured and suggests different ways of doing this. However, the focus here is that development is not evenly spread around the world, and there is a pattern to the distribution of developed and developing countries. In order for pupils to see the pattern, they need to complete the activities, which ask them to colour three maps of world regions according to GNP per capita, population increase and the percentage of primary jobs.

Learning outcomes

By the end of this spread pupils should be able to:

- explain the difference between economic and social indicators of development
- complete maps to show GNP, population increase and the percentage employed in primary jobs for different world regions
- describe the global distribution of richer and poorer regions.

Key vocabulary

- **Gross National Product (GNP)**
- **economic indicators**

Learning objectives

On this spread pupils should learn:

- how development can be measured
- that development is not evenly spread around the world
- that there is a pattern to the distribution of countries with different levels of development.

Skills builder

One of the key skills pupils develop on this spread is the ability to interpret map data (on three maps) and analyse the distribution patterns that their maps show. Pupils are asked:

- whether developing areas are scattered around the world or are grouped together
- whether some continents are more developed than others
- where the more wealthy parts of the world are.

If pupils continue to study geography at GCSE level, they will be expected to describe and explain the reasons for various distribution patterns at a range of different scales from, for example, the distribution of ecosystems to the distribution of earthquakes and volcanic eruptions.

Further discussion suggestions

- What other measures could be used to determine a country's level of development?
- Is wealth the best way of determining a country's level of development?
- Are there likely to be differences in the levels of development between one part of the UK and between different groups of people?

Answers to activities

1 **a** Gross National Product per capita – the wealth of a country: the total amount of money earned by a country in a year divided by its total population.

b Economic indicators of development – measures of development that are based on wealth, e.g. GNP and trade.

c Social indicators of development – development indicators that help to measure standards of living, e.g. school attendance and literacy rates.

2 The UK is a highly developed country, so pupils should reply 'Yes' to this question. Their reasons should include both economic and social examples and should refer to the fact that:

- everyone attends secondary school and should be able to read and write
- people have clean water to drink and sufficient food to eat
- there are plenty of hospitals and everyone has access to good health care, and so on.

Pupil Book pages 98–99

Is development spread evenly? *(continued)*

Answers to activities

3 a Pupils' maps should look like these:

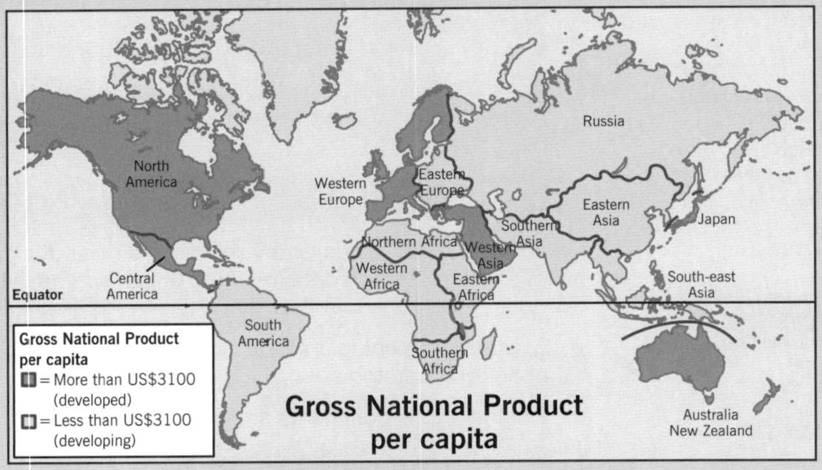

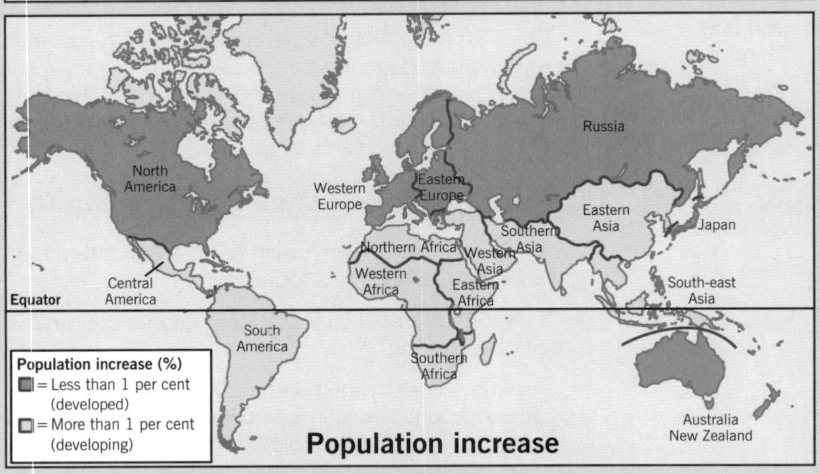

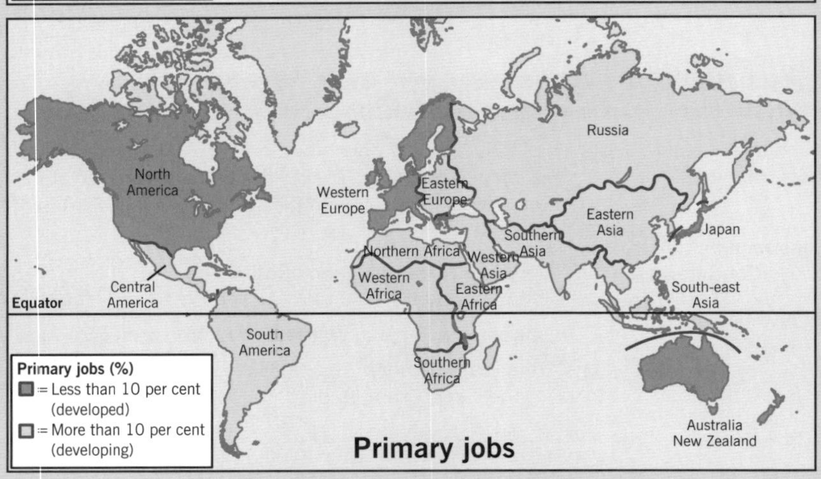

b
- The maps show that developing areas are found grouped together in continents e.g. in South America, Africa, Asia, Russia and Eastern Europe.
- The developed areas of North America and Western Europe are found in the north. Australia and New Zealand are also developed but are in the southern hemisphere.
- Very generally speaking, the north is richer and more developed than the south.

c Pupils could use the map of population increase to draw a line between the developed (richer) areas and developing (poorer) areas. Australia and New Zealand will be included in the developed (richer) areas. Pupils' descriptions of how their line has divided up the world will depend on where they have drawn it.

Pupil Book pages 100–101

How can the rich help the poor?

About this spread

This spread is about aid. Aid is defined in simple terms as a type of help that richer countries give to poorer countries. Aid can be short term or long term and can be given in different ways, such as through the provision of skilled people, equipment, money, and so on. It is important for pupils to understand that the wrong type of aid can be damaging and that the best type of aid schemes should help sustainable development. The provision of a small-scale water supply is given on this spread as an example of an aid scheme that works.

Learning outcomes

By the end of this spread pupils should be able to:

- understand that aid is a form of help usually given by richer countries to poorer countries
- identify the types of aid most suitable for different situations
- decide on a set of rules to ensure that aid is sustainable
- compare an aid scheme with their rules and comment on its success.

Key vocabulary

- **aid**
- **short-term aid**
- **long-term aid**
- **sustainable development**

Learning objectives

On this spread pupils should learn:

- what aid is
- that aid can be short term or long term
- about the different ways in which aid can be given
- that the best aid schemes should be sustainable.

Skills builder

Activity 2 asks pupils to come up with a set of rules that aid schemes should keep to, and list them in order of importance. In other words, they are devising and ranking a set of criteria against which aid schemes can be assessed. The skills being developed here, therefore, are devising the criteria in the first place and then assessing the aid scheme against them.

If pupils continue to study geography at GCSE level, it is likely that they will have to assess various different types of schemes against a range of criteria such as flood prevention schemes, ecotourism projects, and so on.

Further discussion suggestions

- Which global organisations can offer humanitarian aid after disasters such as earthquakes and floods?
- Is giving aid always a good thing?

Answers to activities

1 a

Short-term aid	Long-term aid
Water supply blamed for Ghana disaster	China seeks help for farming problems
Earthquake wrecks Mexico City	Record debts hit Brazilian banks
Crops lost in Bangladesh flood	Massive new health scheme planned for India

b Pupils suggestions should be along the following lines.

- **Earthquake wrecks Mexico City** Emergency assistance such as food, clothing, medical supplies and temporary shelter.
- **Water supply blamed for Ghana disaster** Skilled people, such as engineers, and projects to improve water supplies.
- **Crops lost in Bangladesh flood** Food (either provided free or at a reduced cost).
- **China seeks help for farming problems** Skilled people, such as agricultural experts, and projects to modernise farming.
- **Record debts hit Brazilian banks** Money to help finance improvement schemes and pay for imports.
- **Massive new health scheme planned for India** Skilled people, such as doctors, hospital equipment and money to help finance the scheme.

2 a Pupils should use diagram B to come up with a list of six rules that provison of aid should keep to. They should decide on an order of importance for their list.

b Pupils should assess whether the borehole scheme in photo D meets their rules by answering *Yes*, *No* or *Partly* for each rule.

c Pupils should give the scheme a mark out of ten and write a comment on its success.

Pupil Book pages 102–103

Should we give aid?

About this spread

This spread looks at the issue of giving aid and who gives it (ranging from national governments to charities and international organisations). Pupils are asked to consider different arguments about giving aid, and to decide for themselves whether we should give more aid, less aid or no aid at all to poorer countries. This spread also includes a simple simulation game called 'The road to development?' It shows how development progresses in fits and starts, and is hugely affected by factors outside the control of the country concerned. Population growth, trade and jobs are some of the factors included. Pupils could make their own larger version of the game with a longer road and many more factors.

Learning outcomes

By the end of this spread pupils should be able to:

- identify arguments for and against giving aid
- make a decision about whether aid should be given, and justify their decision
- understand that countries' development does not progress smoothly.

Learning objectives

On this spread pupils should learn:

- that aid is given by different organisations
- that there are arguments for and against giving aid.

Skills builder

The work on aid and development will help pupils to develop their own values and attitudes. They are asked to consider different views on whether or not we should give aid. There is no right or wrong answer, and pupils should be aware that their classmates may have different views to their own. This work will help them to appreciate that it is all right to have different views about issues as long as people have clear, logical and acceptable reasons for their views. They will continue to develop their values and attitudes if they continue to study geography at GCSE level.

Further discussion activities

- How would you respond to television appeals from charities to a natural disaster in a developing country?
- India runs a government space programme, which includes planned human space flight in 2016, as well as satellite launches and missions to the moon and Mars. Its annual budget is $1.32 billion, part funded by the USA. Should India still receive aid?

Answers to activities

1 a Speech bubbles that are **for** giving aid are: B; C; F; H; I. Speech bubbles that are **against** giving aid are: A; D; E; G.

b Pupils should write out the two speech bubbles that they think are the best arguments **for** giving aid and **against** giving aid. The speech bubbles they choose may vary.

c Pupils' views may vary as to whether they think we should give more aid, less aid, or no aid to people who live in countries that have a very low standard of living, but they should give reasons for their answer.

2 a Pupils play the game 'The road to development?' with a partner. Encourage them to think about each of the command squares that they land on.

b

Problems	Help
Cost of imported manufactured goods goes up. World recession closes factories. Foreign banks ask for loan repayment. Rich country ends trade agreement. Crops lost in worst ever flood. Fall in world prices hits export trade. Food shortage causes unrest. Government overthrown.	<u>United Nations aid programme helps with new health scheme.</u> <u>EU advisers help with family-planning programme.</u> <u>Foreign banks give loans for irrigation schemes.</u> Ford open new car factory. Increase in secondary industry jobs. Export of cars and other manufactured goods increased. Money from car sales used for new schools and hospitals. <u>Oxfam sends food to flood disaster area.</u>

Pupil Book pages 104–105

International development enquiry

About this spread

The world development enquiry is intended to be used at the end of the world development unit. It is one of five enquiries in the pupil book, and provides an opportunity to assess pupils' progress.

Learning outcomes

By the end of this spread pupils should be able to:

- assess different development schemes against a range of factors
- choose two schemes to go ahead
- write a report describing the schemes and explaining how they will improve the quality of life for local people.

How can enquiries help with assessment?

For each enquiry in *Interactions* there is a checklist in the appendices. The checklist provides pupils with success criteria so that they know what is expected in order to produce high-quality answers and improve in the future. The checklist can be used in two ways.

- Pupils can use these as they go along, to check that they are meeting the success criteria for the enquiry.
- They can be used for assessment, either by you, as the teacher, or another pupil (for peer marking). Any element that is not ticked provides evidence that the pupil has not met all the criteria.

Learning objectives

On this spread pupils should learn:

- about the aims and approaches of a typical charitable organisation
- about different development schemes
- how to decide which development schemes should go ahead.

What is the world issues enquiry about?

This enquiry begins by telling pupils about a charity LocalAid.

Its aims are to help people in poorer countries improve their standard of living and gain access to their basic rights. Their approach is to support local community groups in setting up and running their own projects. In this enquiry, pupils should imagine they work for a project team in LocalAid Kenya's Nairobi office. Their job is to decide how best to use £50,000 raised by LocalAid and have three proposed development schemes to consider.

In the enquiry, pupils:

- complete a table to show which schemes meet particular factors
- decide which two schemes have the most advantages and consider how they match LocalAid's aims
- decide how to spend the £50,000
- write a report that describes the schemes and explains how they will improve the quality of life for local people. Their explanation should be linked to LocalAid's aims.

Differentiation suggestions

For lower-ability pupils

Work with pupils to make sure they are clear about the steps they need to go through in order to complete the enquiry.

For Activity 2, you could provide pupils with a copy of diagram D. Allow them to highlight the relevant points in different colours to save them having to write out the information.

Provide a writing frame for the report including the headings shown below.

- The need for fair trade
- What a fair trade company needs to do
- What the coffee growers will give in return
- The effects of fair trade on people living in the UK
- The effects of introducing fair trade

For higher-ability pupils

Ask these pupils to find out more information about fair trade by using the Fairtrade website (www.fairtrade.org.uk).

They could find out:

- who needs fair trade
- the range of fair trade products available
- an example of a fair trade producer, and the impact that fair trade has had on the producer. For example, you could suggest investigating the decline of banana farmers in the Windward Islands.

Ask pupils to include this information as part of their report.

Pupil Book pages 106–107

How can we use questions in geography?

About this spread

This spread considers how pupils can find geographical information by asking questions. This is necessary because of the nature of geography as an enquiry-based subject which gives them an active approach to learning.

Learning objectives

On this spread pupils should learn how to:

- ask geographical questions.

Learning outcomes

By the end of this spread pupils should learn:

- to make use of the 'five W's' – 'Who, What, Where, Why and When'
- to make use of 'how' in a geographical question.

Skills builder

It is important that pupils design their own questions as early in the geographical learning process as possible. They should recognise the difference between an open and a closed question. They should learn to make use of questions to elicit knowledge, gain understanding of familiar and unfamiliar circumstances and to appreciate other peoples' attitudes as well as their own values.

Further discussion suggestions

- What questions do I need to ask if I am doing geographical fieldwork outside the classroom?
- How will geographical questions differ when trying to gain understanding rather than merely gaining geographical information?
- In what circumstances are open questions better than closed questions?

Answers to activities

1 **What or where is it?** This is a ski resort situated in a mountain valley.

What is it like? The valley has a flat bottom with steep sides, the lower parts of which are covered in forest. A river flows down the valley. A main road runs down the valley alongside the river. The town has grown up on one side of the valley above which are a number of ski lifts.

Why is it like this? The valley was probably cut by a glacier. The town has grown up on the flatter land because it is easier to build on. The presence of snow means that it has become a centre for winter sports.

How is it changing? The buildings all look modern and there is crane which is being used to build new buildings. This suggests that the growth of the town is recent. The presence of a good road has made the resort accessible and so there are large numbers of cars in the picture.

What have been the effects of these changes? This was once a very remote area and was undisturbed. There will be more air pollution because of the large numbers of cars and buildings which have also had a negative visual impact on the area. Trees may have been cut down to build houses and hotels.

What do you think and feel about the place? *(Answers will vary according to the pupils' opinions.)* The natural beauty of the valley has been spoilt but it may have been difficult to make a living in this area originally. The growth of the resort would have brought money into the area and employment for local people.

2 **Photo on page 44** Possible questions:

Why is there a boat on top of the house? What put it there? Did the boat cause all the damage to the house? What happened to the people living in the house? How long will it take to repair the damage?

Photo on page 45 Possible questions:

What caused all the damage? How many cars were involved? How many people were killed or injured? Why were the trees and the telegraph lines not destroyed? How much is it likely to cost to repair? What were the effects of the people living in the town?

3 Is it an urban or rural area? How many people live in the area? How far is it from the shops? What are the local schools like and how will I get there? What leisure facilities are there nearby?

4

a	Photo B	b Photo C
1	People are standing in a queue.	A lady is being rescued by the fire service.
2	The place has been flooded.	The lady's home has been flooded and she has to be rescued.
3	A tidal wave may have hit the town or there had been very heavy rain.	A river has burst its banks.
4	They look poor and the boy has a bowl, possibly for collecting food.	They would have a good standard of living and have a good level of service.
5	They are desperate because their homes have been destroyed and they are short of food.	It must be satisfying to help people and she is pleased to be rescued.
6	This is in a poor country like Bangladesh.	It is in a developed country like the UK.

c The places shown in photos B and C have both been flooded which causes distress by homes being flooded. In photo B, the people have to look for the basics such as food and water that is also needed by many others. Help has come to the lady in photo C, but it is likely that she will not be short of food and water.

Pupil Book pages 108–109

How can we devise a questionnaire?

About this spread

This spread considers the best way of devising a questionnaire to ensure the results obtained are in a form that could be easily quantified. This will allow the pupils to describe and interpret the results and come to a conclusion following a detailed interrogation of the evidence.

Learning outcomes

By the end of this spread pupils should learn:

- to understand the purpose of a questionnaire
- how to construct a successful questionnaire.

Key vocabulary

- **questionnaire**

Learning objectives

On this spread pupils should learn how to:

- design a questionnaire

Skills builder

Designing a questionnaire will test the pupils' ability to write concisely and to the point, and to identify the most important points i.e. which questions to include. As they will be approaching other people, including the general public, they will learn how to be polite and respectful and to make use of appropriate language when addressing the people being sampled.

Further discussion suggestions

- How many people should there be in your sample?
- What should you try to include in your sample?
- What is the disadvantage of using too small a sample?

Answers to activities

1 **a** On 6 June at 12.30 p.m.

b The information centre.

c By being polite to the person being interviewed and by telling them the reason that you asking the questions.

d 1

e 9

f There is no space for longer answers.

2 1 This is a bad question: it is too vague and it also could give a huge range of answers which would be difficult to analyse. It would be better to have some suggestions to tick, which would be quicker.

2 This is a good question: but it should have boxes to tick.

3 This is a bad question: the obvious answer is 'yes' or 'no' which does not give the information required.

4 This is a bad question: the question is too vague. It would be better to give a list of features that would allow the person to know what you were trying to find out.

5 This is a bad question: the first part is too vague. It would be better to reduce the possible range of values to five or even three. Also the wording could be better. It may be better to ask something along the lines of 'How easy did the person find the parts of the shopping centre that they were looking for?'

3 A wide range of possibilities here, but the questionnaire in drawing A should be used as a model.

Pupil Book pages 110–111

How can we measure shopping quality?

About this spread

This spread introduces the use of an environmental survey to measure shopping quality. It shows how a bipolar or range chart can be used to show a pupil's personal view, as well as the opinions of others. The criteria used to access environmental quality will need to be appropriate to the topic or the area being investigated.

Learning objectives

On this spread pupils should learn:

- what a 'quality of environment survey' is
- that a survey can be used to compare several different shopping areas.

Learning outcomes

By the end of this spread pupils should be able to:

- devise a survey with appropriate criteria that are relevant to the topic or area under investigation
- draw conclusions and make inferences from the resultant survey(s).

Key vocabulary

- **quality of environment (environmental quality) survey**

Skills builder

These surveys give pupils the opportunity to make judgments and to voice opinions. It is important that they do not pick their view from 'out of thin air', but they are able to support their opinions by rational reasons and supporting evidence. Following the completion of an environmental survey there could be the opportunity for pupils to express their views verbally in front of an audience, thus developing their verbal reasoning skills.

Further discussion suggestions

- What criteria would you use when accessing the environmental quality of an area of open space?
- If a scoring system of 1–5 was used to assess the environmental quality of the school grounds what descriptors would you give to each of the values 1–5?

Answers to activities

1 and **2**

There can be a range of answers for the surveys of shopping centres B–D. The pupils should be encouraged to use the full range of values for 1–5.

3 **a** The most likely answer is D.

b The most likely answer is B.

c Possible answers could be:

- plenty of room to walk
- pedestrianised
- places to sit
- trees to give the place some greenery.

d Possible answers could be:

- shops are only small so may be a limited range of things on offer
- there is a car visible so there may be a busy road to cross and there will be traffic noise
- there is no greenery shown
- pavements have notice boards which may get in the way if there are many people trying to shop.

e Plenty of opportunity for pupils to give their ideas here such as pedestrianising the street, adding some pleasant street furniture such as benches. Providing litter bins to keep the area free of litter, etc.

Pupil Book pages 112–113

What is a geographical enquiry?

About this spread

This spread continues the earlier work on the importance of asking geographical questions. This fundamental aspect of effective geographical learning is further developed by showing how the use of questioning can be used in a longer investigation or enquiry, where the title is in the form of a question.

Learning objectives

On this spread pupils should learn:

- that there are distinct stages in writing a geographical enquiry
- that the title can be in the form of an hypothesis or a question.

Learning outcomes

By the end of this spread pupils should be able to:

- devise a meaningful title that lends itself to investigation through a 'route to enquiry'
- that an enquiry can be factual or issue based.

Key vocabulary

- **enquiry**
- **hypothesis**

Skills builder

It is likely that when introducing the process of geographical enquiry for the first time, the pupils will find it easier to have the title in the form of a question. Pupils are used to answering questions and are therefore more likely to be able to come up with an answer that will act as the conclusion to the investigation. It is useful for them to be introduced to the idea of hypothesis testing, in which the title is written as a statement and they are required to collect evidence to prove or disprove the assertion made in the title.

Further discussion suggestions

- What is the difference between primary and secondary pieces of information or data?
- Does all the information collected have to have a numerical value?
- How useful would a photograph, taken for example on a mobile phone, be as a source of information and how could it be used in a geographic enquiry?

Answers to activities

1 Enquiry involves looking for evidence in the form of useful pieces of information. This evidence is then interrogated and conclusions reached.

2 a **Physical** Weather and climate; Farming; Rivers

Human Settlement; Industry; Environmental concerns

Note that there are only six enquiries in total; three physical and three human.

b The answers will depend on the local area of the school.

3 Some examples of issue-based enquiries:

- Should the by-pass follow route A or route B?
- Should the centre of the town be pedestrianised?
- Tourism brings disadvantages to the town.
- The new housing development should not take place at X.

4 a
- The title is often in the form of a hypothesis rather than a question.
- It is concerned with a topic on which there are differences of opinion.
- They are concerned with issues which affect people.
- They require a decision to be made.

b Rivers, industry, environmental concerns.

c Pupils answers will vary. It will depend on the local area.

Pupil Book pages 114–115

What are the key sections of an enquiry?

About this spread

This spread shows how to structure an enquiry so that there is a logical sequence to the investigation. There is a clear 'route to enquiry'.

Learning objectives

On this spread pupils should learn:

- that the write up of an investigation must have a definite structure with distinct sections that follow logically on from each other
- that checklists are useful to ensure each section covers what it is meant to.

Learning outcomes

By the end of this spread pupils should be able to:

- produce a well-argued piece of geographical investigation that has an introduction, a main part and a conclusion
- understand that there needs to be geography underpinning all parts of an enquiry.

Skills builder

Pupils who continue with the subject to GCSE or A Level may well be required to undertake the writing of a geographical enquiry based on their fieldwork. This may be examined as a component in its own right or as the basis of a written examination question. The skills learnt here will serve them in good stead in their future geographical studies.

Further discussion suggestions

- What data presentation techniques could be used to illustrate the data collected?
- What are the key things a graph you draw as part of a geographical enquiry must have?
- Why is rainfall shown as a bar graph but temperature is shown on a line graph?

Answers to activities

1

Introduction	Main part	Conclusion
Starts off the enquiry	Largest section of the enquiry	Links the results to the original aims
Tells the reader what you are going to do	Mixture of written text and data	Answers the question set by the enquiry title
Includes basic information	Includes maps, graphs, drawings and photos	Looks at all the work done

2 This will depend on the topic chosen but it should give the pupil the opportunity to be inventive, perhaps making use of ICT software packages and downloaded illustrations.

Pupil Book pages 116–117

How should an enquiry be presented?

About this spread

This spread outlines the importance of data presentation in a geographical enquiry. Presentations can include graphical, cartographic and photographic techniques. It is emphasised that an enquiry should include a mixture of drawings and text.

Learning objectives

On this spread pupils should learn:

- that their enquiry should be neat and well planned
- that the enquiry should include a mixture of drawings and text.

Learning outcomes

By the end of this spread pupils should be able to:

- use appropriate data presentation techniques to illustrate the data collection
- understand that there is a need for the data presentation techniques to be both accurate and appropriate with all the conventions of a title, scale, and a key where required.

Skills builder

The use of ICT is a tool that will be useful in the presentation of a geographical enquiry. A Microsoft Excel spreadsheet can contain all kinds of data and can create simple graphs from this data. It is important, however, that the pupils use a graph that is appropriate to the data being illustrated as the spreadsheet may produce a graph that is not appropriate to their requirements. The pupils' ICT skills must be such that the pupils are able to give the graph the required conventions mentioned above.

Further discussion suggestions

- What kind of data can be shown on the following data presentation techniques: a line graph, a bar graph, a pie diagram?
- What has to be done to numerical data before a pie diagram can be drawn?
- What is the difference between a label and an annotation on a photograph or sketch?

Answers to activities

1 a Three advantages would be:

- attractive to look at
- easy to read
- easy to make a note of the results.

b Wide margins are needed so that no work is hidden by any binding.

c Figures need to be numbered so when they are discussed in the text the reader knows which figure is being referred to.

d It is useful to plan on rough paper first in order to:

- get things in the correct order
- plan the overall structure of the enquiry.

2 a The title should indicate what aspect of the shop the drawing is trying to illustrate so that the viewer knows what to look for.

b Annotation should be used rather than simple labels.

3
- Has the photo got a title?
- Has the location of the photo been given?
- Is the time, date and year of the photo given?
- Is there an indication of the season (if this is appropriate)?
- Is there some indication of the weather conditions at the time the photo was taken?
- Can an overlay be used to outline the particular parts of the photo which are relevant to the topic of the enquiry?
- Are arrows pointing out significant features or names accurately positioned with the point of the arrow actually touching the feature being indicated?
- Has the photo been given a figure number?
- Have annotations been used rather than simple labels that give some detailed description or interpretation of the feature pointed out?
- Has the photo been referred to in the write-up?

Appendix 1 The environmental regions enquiry checklist

Before you finish your enquiry use the reminders below to make sure that you have covered all of the correct points.

Data collection — Have you

	Student	Assessor
• made a copy of table A	☐	☐
• analysed carefully maps B, D, E and F	☐	☐
• completed columns 1–5 of table A using the information you found?	☐	☐

Name the ecosystems — To succeed make sure you …

	Student	Assessor
• identify trends and patterns in the data, for example wettest, hottest	☐	☐
• read the guide to natural ecosystems (biomes) carefully	☐	☐
• match the data from the table to the guide to natural ecosystems (biomes)	☐	☐
• name each type of vegetation in places A–G.	☐	☐

Data presentation — To succeed make sure you …

	Student	Assessor
• make an accurate copy of figure B	☐	☐
• give your map a key	☐	☐
• include the mountains in your key	☐	☐
• think carefully about your choice of colour	☐	☐
• present your work neatly.	☐	☐

A picture journey — To succeed make sure you …

	Student	Assessor
• make a copy of figure C	☐	☐
• accurately label the seven places at the correct latitudes	☐	☐
• use a simple diagram to show vegetation at each location	☐	☐
• give detailed reasons for the differences in vegetation, including: – latitude – relief – rainfall – temperature.	☐	☐

Question 4 — To really succeed include in your answer:

	Student	Assessor
• temperature range	☐	☐
• seasonality	☐	☐
• hours of sunlight	☐	☐
• drought.	☐	☐

Appendix 2 The volcano enquiry checklist

Before you finish your enquiry use the reminders below to make sure that you have covered all of the correct points.

Section 1 Have you …

	Student	Assessor
• made a copy of table D	☐	☐
• studied the drawing of Mount Etna carefully	☐	☐
• used the key to analyse the drawing	☐	☐
• for each factor in table D scored each route out of 5	☐	☐
• added up the scores for each factor	☐	☐
• put the total scores at the bottom of the table	☐	☐
• checked your calculations	☐	☐

Section 2 To succeed make sure you …

	Student	Assessor
• decide which route you would choose, according to the scores	☐	☐
• write a description of the route you have chosen	☐	☐
• colour code table D to show the advantages and disadvantages	☐	☐
• describe the advantages	☐	☐
• describe the disadvantages	☐	☐
• use evidence from the drawing in all of your answers	☐	☐
• check your spelling, punctuation and grammar.	☐	☐

Section 3 To succeed make sure you …

	Student	Assessor
• describe what *evacuation* means	☐	☐
• decide who needs to be evacuated first	☐	☐
• write your answer using **evidence** and **explaining** your reasons	☐	☐
• decide what they should take with them	☐	☐
• write your answer using **evidence** and **explaining** your reasons	☐	☐
• decide what types of vehicles will be needed	☐	☐
• write your answer using **evidence** and **explaining** your reasons	☐	☐
• decide what items the evacuees will need to make them comfortable	☐	☐
• write your answer using **evidence** and **explaining** your reasons	☐	☐
• check your spelling, punctuation and grammar.	☐	☐

Appendix 3 The resources enquiry checklist

Before you finish your enquiry use the reminders below to make sure that you have covered all of the correct points.

Section 1 Data analysis and evaluation

	Student	Assessor
• Look at map A on page 70 and see what facilities already exist at the reserve.	☐	☐
• Look at the suggestions on page 71 and discuss how best to spend the money.	☐	☐

Section 2 Decision making

Either:	Student
• use your table to help you decide what to spend the money on	☐
• decide which suggestions are best for the nature reserve	☐
• calculate how many of each you can afford.	☐
Or:	
• draw up your own table to help you decide what to spend the money on	☐
• decide which suggestions are best for the nature reserve	☐
• calculate how many of each you can afford.	☐

Putting forward a proposal

You must:	Student	Assessor
• write a report for the project director	☐	☐
• describe what you propose to do	☐	☐
• explain how each of your proposals will improve the reserve	☐	☐
• use the information from your table	☐	☐
• link your answer to the main aims of the project.	☐	☐

Appendix 4 The China enquiry checklist

Section 1 The Introduction

Have you ...	Student	Assessor
• included a title	☐	☐
• defined the terms 'development' and 'standard of living'	☐	☐
• explained how economic factors help to measure development	☐	☐
• explained how social factors help to measure development	☐	☐
• explained how cultural factors help to measure development?	☐	☐

Section 2 The main part

To succeed make sure you ...	Student	Assessor
• have given a heading to each of the drawings numbered 1–9 on page 87	☐	☐
• draw a diagram ranking the different measures as to how well they show whether China is a developed country	☐	☐
• draw three bar graphs to show the figures in drawings 10, 11 and 12 on page 87	☐	☐
• give each graph a title and have correctly labelled the axes.	☐	☐

Section 3 Conclusion

Decide whether the different measures indicate that China is a developed or a developing country by:

	Student	Assessor
• showing if wealth and other economic factors indicate whether or not China is developed	☐	☐
• using social and cultural evidence to show how developed China has become	☐	☐
• showing how China's rapidly growing economy can help it develop	☐	☐
• showing how China's rapidly growing economy can improve its peoples' standard of living.	☐	☐

Extension

	Student	Assessor
• Explain why you put the different measures in the position you did on your diamond diagram.	☐	☐
• Suggest why China has a different position in the tables of wealth, education and food on page 87.	☐	☐

Appendix 5 International development enquiry checklist

Before you finish your enquiry use the reminders below to make sure that you have covered all of the correct points.

Have you ...

	Student	Assessor
• copied table C	☐	☐
• read the proposals carefully	☐	☐
• showed the advantages of each scheme by ticking columns 1, 2 and 3 in table **C**	☐	☐
• decided which two schemes you would choose	☐	☐
• considered how each scheme matches the aims of LocalAid shown in drawing **A**?	☐	☐

To succeed make sure you ...

	Student	Assessor
• copy table D	☐	☐
• list the items and costs for **both** of your schemes	☐	☐
• decide how many of each item you want	☐	☐
• work out the total costs	☐	☐
• ensure your total does not exceed £50,000.	☐	☐

You must ...

• think carefully about the layout of your report	☐	☐
• describe **both** schemes	☐	☐
• explain how they will improve the quality of life for local people	☐	☐
• link your explanation to the aims of LocalAid.	☐	☐

You should ...

• refer to table C in your answer as evidence of how the scheme will improve quality of life.	☐	☐
• refer to table D in your evidence to show exactly what you will spend the money on.	☐	☐

You could ...

• include an annotated sketch map to show where the schemes will be located.	☐	☐